# Advances in Computer Vision and Pattern Recognition

AF837468

For further volumes:
www.springer.com/series/4205

Hong Cheng

# Autonomous Intelligent Vehicles

## Theory, Algorithms, and Implementation

Springer

Prof. Hong Cheng
School of Automation Engineering
University of Electronic Science and Technology
610054 Chengdu, Sichuan,
People's Republic of China
hcheng@uestc.edu.cn

*Series Editors*
Professor Sameer Singh, PhD
Research School of Informatics
Loughborough University
Loughborough
UK

Dr. Sing Bing Kang
Microsoft Research
Microsoft Corporation
One Microsoft Way
Redmond, WA 98052
USA

ISSN 2191-6586 e-ISSN 2191-6594
Advances in Computer Vision and Pattern Recognition
ISBN 978-1-4471-2279-1 e-ISBN 978-1-4471-2280-7
DOI 10.1007/978-1-4471-2280-7
Springer London Dordrecht Heidelberg New York

British Library Cataloguing in Publication Data
A catalogue record for this book is available from the British Library

Library of Congress Control Number: 2011943117



Printed on acid-free paper

Springer is part of Springer Science+Business Media (www.springer.com)

# Preface

Over the years, the field of intelligent vehicles has become a major research theme in intelligent transportation systems since traffic accidents are serious and growing problems all over the world. The goal of an intelligent vehicle is to augment vehicle autonomous driving either entirely or partly for the purposes of safety, comfortability, and saving energy. Indeed, many technologies of intelligent vehicles root in autonomous mobile robots. The tasks of intelligent vehicles become even more challenging compared to indoor mobile robots for two reasons. First, real-time dynamic complex environment perception and modeling will challenge current indoor robot technologies. Autonomous intelligent vehicles have to finish the basic procedures: perceiving and modeling environment, localizing and building maps, planning paths and making decisions, and controlling the vehicles within limit time for real-time purposes. Meanwhile, we face the challenge of processing large amounts of data from multi-sensors, such as cameras, lidars, radars. This is extremely hard in more complex outdoor environments. Toward this end, we have to implement those tasks in more efficient ways. Second, vehicle motion control faces the challenges of strong nonlinear characteristics due to high mass, especially in the processes of high speed and sudden steering. In this case, both lateral and longitudinal control algorithms of indoor robots do not work well.

This book presents our recent research work on intelligent vehicles and is aimed at the researchers and graduate students interested in intelligent vehicles. Our goal in writing this book is threefold. First, it creates an updated reference book of intelligent vehicles. Second, this book not only presents object/obstacle detection and recognition, but also introduces vehicle lateral and longitudinal control algorithms, which benefits the readers keen to learn broadly about intelligent vehicles. Finally, we put emphasis on high-level concepts, and at the same time provide the low-level details of implementation. We try to link theory, algorithms, and implementation to promote intelligent vehicle research.

This book is divided into four parts. The first part **Autonomous Intelligent Vehicles** presents the research motivation and purposes, the state-of-art of intelligent vehicles research. Also, we introduce the framework of intelligent vehicles. The second part **Environment Perception and Modeling** which includes *Road detection* *and tracking*, *Vehicle detection and tracking*, *Multiple-sensor based multiple-object tracking* introduces environment perception and modeling. The third part **Vehicle Localization and Navigation** which includes *An integrated DGPS/IMU positioning approach*, *Vehicle navigation using global views* presents vehicle navigation based on integrated GPS and INS. The fourth part **Advanced Vehicle Motion control** introduces vehicle lateral and longitudinal motion control.

Most of this book refers to our research work at Xi'an Jiaotong University and Carnegie Mellon University. During the last ten years of research, a large number of people had been working in the Springrobot Project at Xi'an Jiaotong University. I would like to deliver my deep respect to my Ph.D advisor, Professor Nanning Zheng, who leaded me into this field. Also I would like to thank: Yuehu Liu, Xiaojun Lv, Lin Ma, Xuetao Zhang, Junjie Qin, Jingbo Tang, Yingtuan Hou, Jing Yang, Li Zhao, Chong Sun, Fan Mu, Ran Li, Weijie Wang, and Huub van de Wetering. Also, I would like to thank Jie Yang at Carnegie Mellon University who supported Hong Cheng's research work during his stay at this university and Zicheng Liu at Microsoft Research who helped Hong Cheng discuss vehicle navigation with global views. I also would like to our sincere and deep thanks to Zhongjun Dai who helped immensely with figure preparation and with the typesetting of the book in LaTeX. Many people have helped by proofreading draft materials and providing comments and suggestions, including Nana Chen, Rui Huang, Pingxin Long, Wenjun Jing, Yuzhuo Wang. Springer has provided excellent support throughout the final stages of preparation of this book, and I would like to thank our commissioning editor Wayne Wheeler for his support and professionalism as well as Simon Rees for his help.

Chengdu, People's Republic of China Hong Cheng

# Contents

# Part I
# Autonomous Intelligent Vehicles

# Chapter 1
# Introduction

## 1.1 Research Motivation and Purpose

Autonomous intelligent vehicles are generic technology sets to augment vehicle autonomous driving entirely or in part for autonomous and safety purposes. Fundamentally, autonomous intelligent vehicles refer to many mobile robot technologies. In principle, we consider autonomous intelligent vehicles as mobile robot platforms in this book. Hence, an intelligent vehicle consists of four fundamental technologies: environment perception and modeling, localization and map building, path planning and decision-making, and motion control [26], shown in Fig. 1.1.

The dreams of a human being are the power and source of pushing the world forward. The National Research Council once predicted that the core weapon in the twentieth century would be the tank, while that in the twenty-first century—an unmanned battle system [1]. Moreover, a third of the U.S. military ground vehicles must be unmanned by 2015. Therefore, since 1980s, the Defense Advanced Research Projects Agency (DARPA) initiated a new project, namely the unmanned battle project. Its goal is to design a car which can autonomously implement navigation, obstacle avoidance, and path planning. Afterwards, it opened an intelligent vehicle era. Moreover, the U.S. Department of Energy launched a ten year robot and intelligent system plan (1986–1995), and also the space robot plan. In terms of space exploration, the National Aeronautics and Space Administration (NASA) has developed several wheeled rovers, such as Spirit and Opportunity, for science explorations.[1]

A major concern associated with the rapid growth in automotive production is an increase in traffic congestion and accidents [36]. To solve the problem, the governments all over the world have been increasing funds to improve the traffic infrastructure, enforce traffic laws, and educate drivers about traffic regulations. In addition, research institutes have launched R&D projects in driver assistance and safety warning systems. Therefore, in the last decade, many research works in the

[1] http://marsrovers.jpl.nasa.gov/overview/.

H. Cheng, *Autonomous Intelligent Vehicles*,
Advances in Computer Vision and Pattern Recognition,
DOI 10.1007/978-1-4471-2280-7_1, 

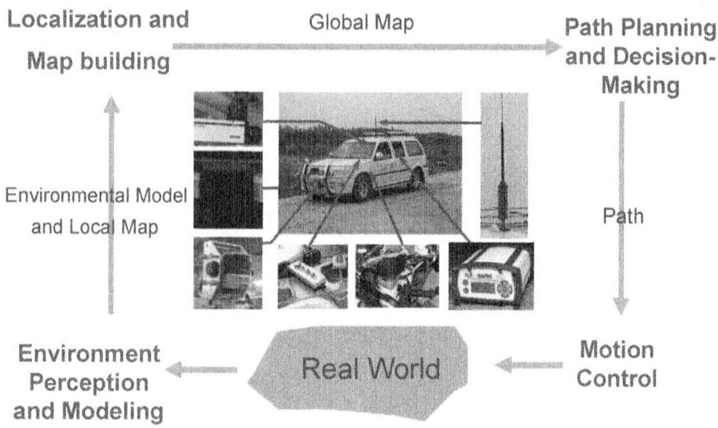


**Fig. 1.1** The basic framework of autonomous intelligent vehicles

area of intelligent vehicles all over the world led to Intelligent Transportation Systems (ITS) for improving road safety and reducing traffic accidents [7]. Autonomous intelligent vehicles are now widely applied to Driver Assistance and Safety Warning Systems (DASWS) [36], such as Forward Collision Warning [9, 27], Adaptive Cruise Control [32], Lane Departure Warning [16]. In recent years, with the development of economy and society, the issues of traffic safety, energy shortage, and environment pollution became more serious. Those problems then led to higher volumes of research and applications. Toward this end, combining vehicles, drivers and lanes together, we can implement better traffic capacity and traffic safety using computer control, artificial intelligence and communication technologies [3].

The most important reasons for the large numbers of traffic accidents are burdensome driving and fatigue driving. When driving on the traffic congestion lanes, drivers have to do a lot of operations, such as shifting and pulling clutches, and they have to complete 20 to 30 coordination operations of hand and foot movements each minute. With the economic development and the increase of vehicle ownership, the number of non-professional drivers are rising, leading to frequent traffic accidents. As a result, traffic accidents have become the first public nuisance in modern society. Traffic problems have troubled the whole world, and then, the question of how to improve traffic safety has become an urgent social issue. Lane departure systems, fatigue detection systems, and automatic cruise control can greatly reduce driver's workload and improve transportation system safety.

The widely application prospects of intelligent vehicles promote the development of transportation systems which attracts a growing number of research institutions and auto manufacturers. The DARPA had held the Grand Challenges and the Urban Challenge since 2004. Their goal is to develop autonomous intelligent vehicles capable of both perceiving various environments, such as desert trails, roads, and urban areas, and navigating at high speeds[2] [5, 30, 31]. In the first Grand Chal-

[2]http://www.urban-challenge.com/_eng/.

lenge, CMU's Sandstorm went for 7.4 miles from the start, opening the possibilities of autonomous capability [30]. In 2005, five vehicles, namely Stanley, Sandstorm, High lander, Kat-5, and TerraMax, were able to complete that challenge, and Stanley took the first place ahead of Sandstorm [31]. After the success of the two Grand Challenges, the DARPA organized the Urban Challenge [5]. In the Urban Challenge, based on the technical reports of implementing safe and capable autonomous vehicles, the DARPA allowed 53 teams to demonstrate how they navigate simple urban driving scenes. After these demonstrations, only 36 teams were invited to attend the National Qualification Event (NQE). Finally, only 11 teams were qualified for the Urban Challenge Final Event (UCFE). In China, the 2008 Beijing Olympic Games whose slogans were Hi-tech Olympics and Green Olympics adopted many advanced traffic management systems, intelligent vehicles, electric vehicles for improving vehicle safety performance, reducing pollution, easing traffic congestion. Consequently, those innovations drew attention of many researchers. In 2011, China released ten leading edge technologies and modern transportation technologies among which were technologies aiming at developing intelligent vehicles. Moreover, the National Natural Science Foundation of China launched the state key development plan in 2008, so that audio-visual information based cognizing computation[3] could integrate human–computer interfaces, computer vision, language understanding, and cooperative computing. Finally, upon those achievements, the goal of this plan is to develop autonomous intelligent vehicles which are capable of both perceiving natural environment and making intelligent decisions. Meanwhile, similar to the Grand Challenge supported by DARPA, the plan holds the Future Challenge each year.

The research on intelligent vehicles can greatly facilitate the rapid development of other disciplines, such as exploring planets. The U.S. Mars vehicles Spirit and Opportunity play an irreplaceable role in exploring Mars and the vast universe beyond Mars [13, 23]. In China, the government released the White Paper "China Aerospace" in November 2000, which targets exploring the moon and other planets in the near future. Furthermore, space mobile robots are the key part for exploring planets which could benefit the utilizing solar energy.

## 1.2 The Key Technologies of Intelligent Vehicles

As we mentioned before, intelligent vehicles are a set of intelligent agents which integrate multi-sensor fusion based environment perception and modeling, localization and map building, path planning and decision-making, and motion control, shown in Fig. 1.1. The environment perception and modeling module is responsible for sensing environment structures in a multi-sensor way and providing a model of the surrounding environment. Here, the environment model includes a list of moving objects, that of static obstacles, vehicle position relative to the current road, the

[3]http://ccvai.xjtu.edu.cn.

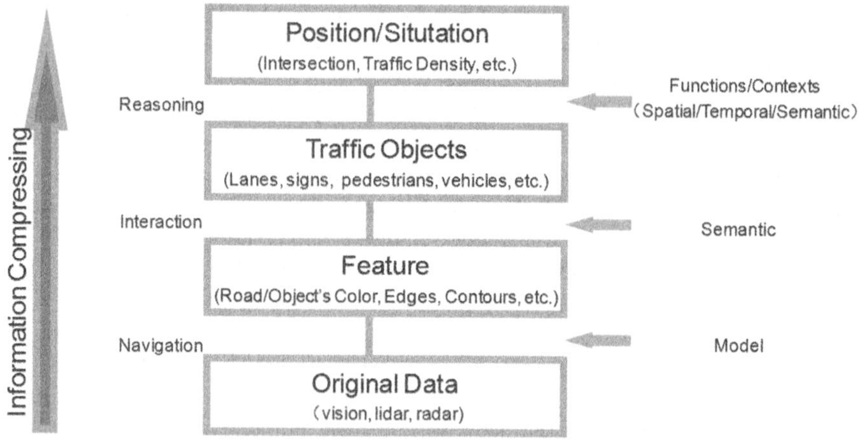


**Fig. 1.2** Multi-sensor fusion based modeling and environment perception

road shape, etc. Finally, this module provides the environment model and the local map to the localization and map building module by processing the original data, vision, lidar, and radar. The second module, vehicle localization and map building, is to use geometric feature location estimate in the map to determine the vehicle's position, and to interpret sensor information to estimate the locations of geometric features in a global map. As a result, the second module yields a global map based on the environment model and a local map. The path planning and decision-making module is to assist in ensuring that the vehicle is operated in accordance with the rules of the ground, safety, comfortability, vehicle dynamics, and environment contexts. Hence, this module can potentially improve mission efficiency and generate the desired path. The final module, motion control, is to execute the commands necessary to achieve the planned paths, thus yielding interaction between the vehicle and its surrounding environment. A brief introduction of these modules is presented below.

### *1.2.1 Multi-sensor Fusion Based Environment Perception and Modeling*

Figure 1.2 illustrates a general environment perception and modeling framework. From this framework, we can see that: (i) The original data are collected by various sensors; (ii) Various features are extracted from the original data, such as road (object) colors, lane edges, building contours; (iii) Semantic objects are recognized using classifiers, and consist of lanes, signs, vehicles, pedestrians; (iv) We can deduce driving contexts, and vehicle positions.

1. Multi-sensor fusion

   Multi-sensor fusion is the basic framework of intelligent vehicles for better sensing surrounding environment structures, and detecting objects/obstacles. Roughly, the sensors used for surrounding environment perception are divided into two categories: active and passive ones. Active sensors include lidar, radar, ultrasonic and radio, while the commonly-used passive sensors are infrared and visual cameras. Different sensors are capable of providing different detection precision and range, and yielding different effects on environment. That is, combining various sensors could cover not only short-range but also long-range objects/obstacles, and also work in various weather conditions. Furthermore, the original data of different sensors can be fused in low-level fusion, high-level fusion, and hybrid fusion [4, 14, 20, 35].
2. Dynamic Environment Modeling

   Dynamic environment modeling based on moving on-vehicle cameras plays an important role in intelligent vehicles [17]. However, this is extremely challenging due to the combined effects of ego-motion, blur, light changing. Therefore, traditional methods for gradual illumination change, small motion objects [28] such as background subtraction, do not work well any more, even those that have been widely used in surveillance applications. Consequently, more and more approaches try to handle these issues [2, 17]. Unfortunately, it is still an open problem to reliably model and update background.

   To select different driving strategies, several broad scenarios are usually considered in path planning and decision-making, when navigating roads, intersections, parking lots, jammed intersections. Hence, scenario estimators are helpful for further decision-making, which is commonly used in the Urban Challenge.
3. Object Detection and Tracking

   In general, in a driving environment, we are interested in static/dynamic obstacles, lane markings, traffic signs, vehicles, and pedestrians. Correspondingly, object detection and tracking are the key parts of environment perception and modeling.

### 1.2.2 Vehicle Localization and Map Building

The goal of vehicle localization and map building is to generate a global map by combining the environment model, a local map and global information. In autonomous driving, vehicle localization is either to estimate road geometry or to localize the vehicle relative to roads under the conditions of known maps or unknown maps. Hence, vehicle localization refers to road shape estimation, position filtering, transforming the vehicle pose into a coordinate frame. For vehicle localization, we face several challenges as follows: (i) Usually, the absolute positions from GPS/DGPS and its variants are insufficient due to signal transmission; (ii) The path planning and decision-making module needs more than just the vehicle absolute position as input; (iii) Sensor noises greatly affect the accuracy of vehicle localization. Regarding the first issue, though the GPS and its variants have been widely

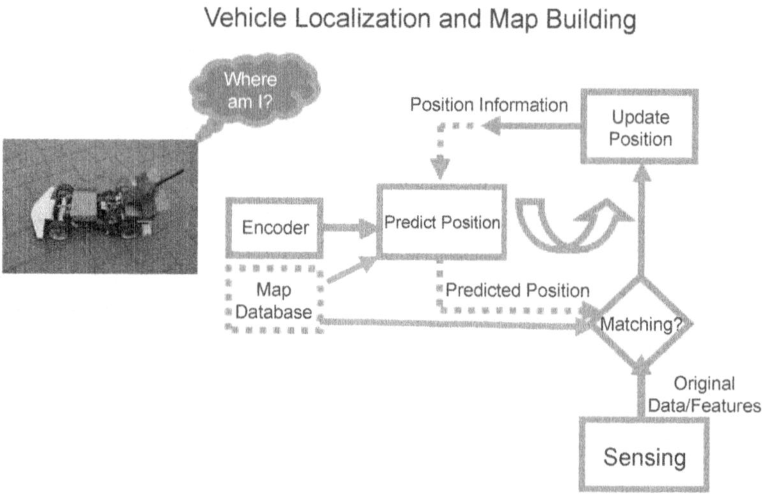


**Fig. 1.3** The framework of vehicle localization and navigation

used in vehicle localization, its performance could degrade due to signal blockages and reflections of buildings and trees. In the worst case, Inertia Navigation System (INS) can maintain a position solution. As for the second issue, local maps fusing laser, radar, and vision data with vehicle states are used to locate and track both static/dynamic obstacles and lanes. Furthermore, global maps could contain lane geometric information, lane makings, step signs, parking lots, check points and provide global environment information. Referring to the third issue, various noise modules are considered to reduce localization error [26].

Map building using various sensors has been addressed by many researchers [18, 22], and it needs to yield the interpretation for the sensor information. Intelligent vehicles could be navigated under the conditions of either known maps or unknown maps. For example, the DARPA Grand Challenge provided the Route Network Definition File (RNDF), which belongs to the case of known maps. However, in exploring Mars, intelligent vehicles could not have the maps of Mars beforehand. This problem is formulated as localizing vehicles traveling in an unknown environment. In this problem, we will handle the dual task of localizing the vehicle and simultaneously modeling the environment, a.k.a., Simultaneous Localization and Map Building (SLAM) [8]. Figure 1.3 illustrates the framework of vehicle localization in an iterated way.

### *1.2.3 Path Planning and Decision-Making*

For the purpose of safe and energy saving navigation, vehicles try to find an optimal path in 2D/3D road space from the initial position to the target position avoiding both static and dynamic obstacle collisions. Hence, global path planning is to

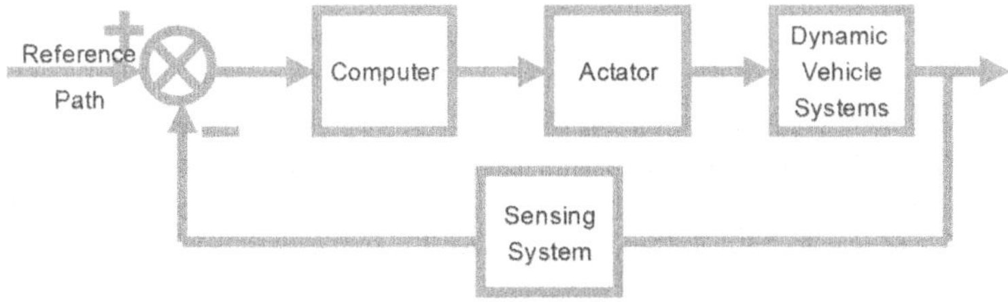


**Fig. 1.4** The framework of vehicle motion control

find the fastest and safest way to get from the initial position to the goal position, while local path planning is to avoid obstacles for safe navigation [6, 11]. Decision-making consists of mission planning and behavioral reasoning. When a vehicle autonomously navigates through the environment, the mission planner incorporates the new observation, thus updating the local maps. Afterwards, the mission planner generates a new rule. The behavioral planner implements behavioral reasoning and the rule generated by the mission planner. Hence, those functions consist of road following, making lane-changes, parking, obstacle avoidance, recovering from abnormal conditions. In many cases, decision-making depends of context driving, especially in driver assistance systems [10].

### *1.2.4 Low-Level Motion Control*

The problem of investigating vehicle lateral and longitudinal control has stimulated significant research work in the last two decades. Its typical applications consist of automatic vehicle following/platoon [12, 29], Adaptive Cruise Control (ACC) [25, 33], lane following [21]. Vehicle control can be broadly divided into two categories: lateral control and longitudinal control [19] (Fig. 1.4). The longitudinal control [29] is related to distance–velocity control between vehicles for safety and comfort purposes. Here some assumptions are made about the state of vehicles and the parameters of models, such as in the PATH project [12]. The lateral control is to maintain the vehicle's position in the lane center, and it can be used for vehicle guidance assistance [15, 34]. Moreover, it is well known that the lateral and longitudinal dynamics of a vehicle are coupled in a combined lateral and longitudinal control, where the coupling degree is a function of the tire and vehicle parameters [24, 34]. In general, there are two different approaches to design vehicle controllers. One way to do this is to mimic driver operations, and the other is based on vehicle dynamic models and control strategies.

## 1.3 The Organization of This Book

This book consists of four parts. The first part is a basic introduction about intelligent vehicles. Furthermore, Chapter 1 introduces the research motivation and purpose, the key technologies. Chapter 2 presents the state-of-the-art of intelligent vehicles in the USA. Chapter 3 introduces the proposed basic framework of intelligent vehicles. The second part presents environment perception and modeling. Chapter 4 presents road detection and tracking algorithms for structured and unstructured roads. Chapter 5 presents on-road vehicle detection and tracking algorithms using Boosted Gabor Features. Chapter 6 introduces a multiple-sensor based multiple-object tracking approach. The third part is about vehicle localization and navigation. Chapter 7 introduces an integrated DGPS/IMU positioning approach. Chapter 8 presents a vehicle navigation approach using global views. The final part is about advanced vehicle motion control. In Chapter 9, a lateral control approach is introduced. In the final chapter, a longitudinal control approach is presented.

## References


1. National Research Council (US) Board on Army Science, National Research Council (US) Commission on Engineering, Technical Systems: Star 21: strategic technologies for the army of the twenty-first century. National Academies (1993)
2. Betke, M., Haritaoglu, E., Davis, L.S.: Real-time multiple vehicle detection and tracking from a moving vehicle. Mach. Vis. Appl., **12**(2), 69–83 (2000)
3. Broggi, A.: Automatic Vehicle Guidance: the Experience of the ARGO Autonomous Vehicle. World Scientific, Singapore (1999)
4. Brooks, R., Iyengar, S.: Multi-sensor Fusion: Fundamentals and Applications with Software. Prentice-Hall, New York (1998)
5. Buehler, M., Iagnemma, K., Singh, S.: Special issue on the 2007 DARPA Urban Challenge, Part II. J. Field Robot., **25**(9), 567–724 (2008)
6. Carsten, J., Rankin, A., Ferguson, D., Stentz, A.: Global path planning on board the Mars exploration rovers. In: Proc. of the IEEE Aerospace Conference (2007)
7. Cheng, H., Zheng, N., Qin, J.: Pedestrian detection using sparse gabor filter and support vector machine. In: Proc. of the IEEE Intelligent Vehicles Symposium (2005)
8. Csorba, M.: Simultaneous localisation and map building. Robotic Recherche Group Department of Engineering of Oxford
9. Dagan, E., Mano, O., Stein, G.P., Shashua, A.: Forward collision warning with a single camera. In: IEEE Intelligent Vehicles Symposium (2004)
10. Fletcher, L., Zelinsky, A.: Context sensitive driver assistance based on gaze–road scene correlation. In: Experimental Robotics. Springer, Berlin (2008)
11. Giesbrecht, J.: Global path planning for unmanned ground vehicles. Technical report, Defense Research and Development Suffield (Alberta) (2004)
12. Godbole, D.N., Lygeros, J.: Longitudinal control of the lead car of a platoon. IEEE Trans. Veh. Technol., **43**(4), 1125–1135 (1994)
13. Hayati, S., Volpe, R., Backes, P., Balaram, J., Welch, R., Ivlev, R., Tharp, G., Peters, S., Ohm, T., Petras, R., et al.: The Rocky 7 Rover: a Mars science craft prototype. In: Proc. of the IEEE International Conference on Robotics and Automation, vol. 3, pp. 2458–2464 (1997)
14. Herpel, T., Lauer, C., German, R., Salzberger, J.: Multi-sensor data fusion in automotive applications. In: IEEE International Conference on Sensing Technology (2008)
15. Hoc, J., Mars, F., Milleville-Pennel, I., Jolly, E., Netto, M., Blosseville, J.: Evaluation of human-machine cooperation modes in car driving for safe lateral control in bends: function delegation and mutual control modes. Le Travail Humain, **69**, 115–185 (2006)
16. Lee, J.W.: A machine vision system for lane-departure detection. Comput. Vis. Image Underst., **86**(1), 52–78 (2002)

17. Leibe, B., Cornelis, N., Cornelis, K., Van Gool, L.: Dynamic 3D scene analysis from a moving vehicle. In: IEEE Conference on Computer Vision and Pattern Recognition (2007)
18. Leonard, J.J., Durrant-Whyte, H.F.: Directed Sonar Sensing for Mobile Robot Navigation. Springer, Berlin (1992)
19. Li, L., Wang, F.Y.: Advanced Motion Control and Sensing for Intelligent Vehicles. Springer, Berlin (2007)
20. Moravec, H.P.: Sensor fusion in certainty grids for mobile robots. AI Mag., **9**(2), 61 (1988)
21. O'Brien, R., Iglesias, P., Urban, T.: Vehicle lateral control for automated highway systems. IEEE Trans. Control Syst. Technol., **4**(3), 266–273 (1996)
22. Pagac, D., Nebot, E.M., Durrant-Whyte, H.: An evidential approach to map-building for autonomous vehicles. IEEE Trans. Robot. Autom. **14**(4), 623–629 (1998)
23. Paris, A., Adonis, C.: Exploring Mars using intelligent robots. Technical report (1995)
24. Pham, H., Hedrick, K., Tomizuka, M.: Combined lateral and longitudinal control of vehicles for IVHS. In: American Control Conference. IEEE, New York (1994).
25. Rajamani, R., Zhu, C.: Semi-autonomous adaptive cruise control systems. IEEE Trans. Veh. Technol., **51**(5), 1186–1192 (2002)
26. Siegwart, R., Nourbakhsh, I.R.: Introduction to Autonomous Mobile Robots. MIT Press, Cambridge (2004)
27. Srinivasa, N.: Vision-based vehicle detection and tracking method for forward collision warning in automobiles. In: IEEE Intelligent Vehicle Symposium (2002)
28. Stauffer, C., Grimson, W.E.L.: Adaptive background mixture models for real-time tracking. In: IEEE Computer Society Conference on Computer Vision and Pattern Recognition (1999)
29. Swaroop, D., Hedrick, J.K., Choi, S.: Direct adaptive longitudinal control of vehicle platoons. IEEE Trans. Veh. Technol., **50**(1), 150–161 (2001)
30. Urmson, C., Anhalt, J., Clark, M., Galatali, T., Gonzalez, J.P., Gowdy, J., Gutierrez, A., Harbaugh, S., Johnson-Roberson, M., Kato, H., et al.: High speed navigation of unrehearsed terrain: Red team technology for grand challenge 2004. CMU-RI Tech. Rep. (2004)
31. Urmson, C., Ragusa, C., Ray, D., Anhalt, J., Bartz, D., Galatali, T., Gutierrez, A., Johnston, J., Harbaugh, S., et al.: A robust approach to high-speed navigation for unrehearsed desert terrain. J. Field Robot., **23**(8), 467–508 (2006)
32. Vahidi, A., Eskandarian, A.: Research advances in intelligent collision avoidance and adaptive cruise control. IEEE Trans. Intell. Transp. Syst., **4**(3), 143–153 (2003)
33. Van Arem, B., Van Driel, C.J.G., Visser, R.: The impact of cooperative adaptive cruise control on traffic-flow characteristics. IEEE Trans. Intell. Transp. Syst., **7**(4), 429–436 (2006)
34. Weilkes, M., Burkle, L., Rentschler, T., Scherl, M.: Future vehicle guidance assistance-combined longitudinal and lateral control. Automatisierungstechnik, **53**(1), 4–10 (2005)
35. Wu, H., Siegel, M., Stiefelhagen, R., Yang, J.: Sensor fusion using Dempster–Shafer theory. In: IEEE Instrumentation and Measurement Technology Conference Proceedings (2002)
36. Zheng, N., Tang, S., Cheng, H., Li, Q., Lai, G., Wang, F.W.: Toward intelligent driver-assistance and safety warning system. IEEE Intell. Syst., **19**(2), 8–11 (2004)

# Chapter 2
# The State-of-the-Art in the USA

## 2.1 Introduction

The field of intelligent vehicles is rapidly growing all over the world, both in the diversity of applications and research [3, 8, 18]. Especially in the U.S., government agencies, universities, and companies working on this hope to develop autonomous driving entirely or in part for safety and for saving more energy. Many previous technologies, such as seat belts, air bags, work only after a traffic accident. Only intelligent vehicles can stop traffic accidents from happening in the first place. Therefore, DARPA has organized the Grand Challenges and the Urban Challenge from 2004 to 2007, which remarkably promoted the technologies of intelligent vehicles around the world. Hence, this chapter presents an overview of the most advanced intelligent vehicle projects which once attended either the Grand Challenges or the Urban Challenge supported by the DARPA in the USA.

## 2.2 Carnegie Mellon University—Boss

The research groups at Carnegie Mellon University had developed the Navlab series [8, 17], from Navlab 1 to 11, which include robot cars, tracks, and buses. The Navlab's applications have included Supervised Classification Applied to Road Following (SCARF) [6, 7], Yet Another Road Following (YARF) [12], Autonomous Land Vehicle In a Neural Net (ALVINN) [11], Rapidly Adapting Lateral Position Handler (RALPH) system [16]. In addition, Sandstorm is an autonomous vehicle which was modified from the High Mobility Multipurpose Wheeled Vehicle (HMMWV) and competed in the DARPA Grand Challenge in 2005. The Highlander is another autonomous vehicle modified from HMMWV H1 which competed in same competition in 2005.

Nevertheless, the latest intelligent vehicle is the Boss system (shown in Fig. 2.1) which won the first place in 2007 Grand Challenge [18]. Boss combines various active and passive sensors to provide faster and safer autonomous driving in an urban

H. Cheng, *Autonomous Intelligent Vehicles*,
Advances in Computer Vision and Pattern Recognition,
DOI 10.1007/978-1-4471-2280-7_2, 

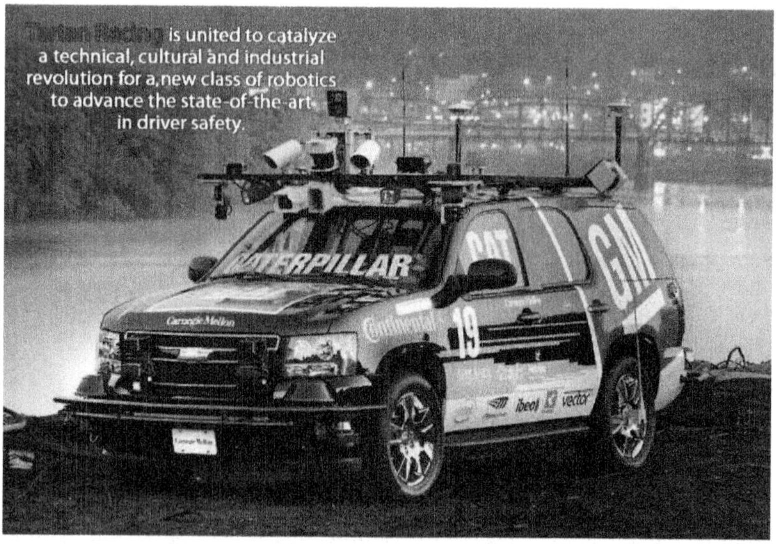


**Fig. 2.1** The intelligent vehicle, named Boss, developed by Carnegie Mellon University's Red Team (published courtesy of Carnegie Mellon University)

environment. Active sensors include lidar and radar, and passive sensors include the Point Grey high-dynamic-range camera. The following functional modules were implemented on the Boss vehicle:

1. Environment perception: Basically, the perception module provides a list of tracked moving objects, static obstacles in a regular grid, and vehicle localization relative to roads, road shape, etc. Furthermore, this module consists of four subsystems, moving obstacle detection and tracking, static obstacle detection and tracking, roadmap localization, and road shape estimation.
2. A three-layer planning system consisting of mission, behavioral, and motion planning is used to drive in urban environments. Mission planning is to detect obstacles and plan new route to its goal. Here, given Road Network Definition File (RNDF) encoding environment connectivity, a cost graph guides vehicles to travel on a road/lane planned by the behavioral subsystem. A value function is calculated to both provide the path from each way point to target way point, and allow the navigation system to respond when an error occurs. Furthermore, Boss is capable of planning another route if there is a blockage.

The behavioral subsystem is in charge of executing the rules generated by the mission planning. In details, this subsystem makes decisions on lane-change, precedence, and safety decisions on different driving contexts, such as roads, intersections. Furthermore, this subsystem needs to complete the tasks, including carrying out the rules generated by the previous mission planner, responding to abnormal conditions, and identifying driving contexts, roads, interactions, and zones. Furthermore, these driving contexts correspond to different behavior strategies consisting of lane driving, intersection handling, and achieving a zone pose. The third layer

**Fig. 2.2** The Stanford University's intelligent vehicle Junior that was the runner-up in the 2007 DARPA Urban Challenge (published courtesy of Stanford University)

of the planning system is the motion planning subsystem which consists of trajectory generation, on-road navigation, and zone navigation. This layer is responsible for executing the current motion goal from the behavior subsystem. In general, this subsystem generates a path towards the target, and tracks the path.

## 2.3 Stanford University—Junior

The Stanford University's research team on intelligent vehicles has been one of the most experienced and successful research labs in the world. To better study and promote the applications of autonomous intelligent vehicles, the Volkswagen group founded the Volkswagen Automotive Innovation Laboratory (VAIL). Until now, Stanford University collaborated with the Volkswagen Group and built several intelligent vehicles, the Stanley (the autonomous Volkswagen Touareg that won the DARPA Grand Challenge in 2005 [10]), Junior (the autonomous Volkswagen Passat that was the runner-up in 2007 DARPA Urban Challenge [14]). Moreover, Google has licensed the sensing technology from Stanley to map out 3D digital cities all over the world. We will introduce Junior that participated in the 2007 Urban Challenge below.

Junior [14], shown in Fig. 2.2, is a modified 2006 Volkswagen Passat wagon, equipped with five laser range finders, a GPS/INS, five radars, two Intel quad core computer systems, and a custom drive-by-wire interface. Hence, this vehicle is capable of detecting an obstacle up to 120 m away.

Junior's software architecture is designed as a data-driven pipeline and consists of five modules:

- Sensor interface: This interface provides data for other modules.
- Perception modules: These modules segment sensor data into moving vehicles and static obstacles, and also provide accurate position relative to the digital map of the environment.
- Navigation modules: These modules consist of motion planners, a hierarchical finite state machine, and generate the behavior of the vehicle.
- Drive-by-wire interface: This interface receives the control commands from navigation modules, and enables the control of throttles, brakes, steering wheels, gear shifting, turn signals, and emergency brake.
- Global services: The system can provide logging, time stamping, message-passing support, and watch-dog functions to keep the system running reliably.

Furthermore, we introduce three fundamental modules: environment perception, precision localization, and navigation. In the perception module, there are two basic functions, static/dynamic obstacle detection and tracking, RNDF localization and update, where lasers implement primary scanning, and a radar system works as an early warning for moving objects in intersections as complement. After perceiving traffic environment, Junior estimates a local alignment between a digital map in the RNDF form and its current position from local sensors. In navigation module, the first task is to plan global paths, where there are two navigation cases, road navigation and free-style navigation. However, basic navigation modules do not include intersections. Furthermore, Junior strives to prevent itself from getting stuck in behavior hierarchy.

Nowadays, researchers at Stanford University are still working on autonomous parking in tight parking spots[1] and autonomous valet parking.

## 2.4 Virginia Polytechnic Institute and State University—Odin

The team VictorTango formed by Virginia Tech and TORC Technologies developed Odin[2] [2], which took the third place in 2004 DARPA Grand Challenge. The Odin consists of three main parts: base vehicle body, perception, and planning.

Now, we introduce the base vehicle platform. Odin is a modified 2005 Hybrid Ford Escape, shown in Fig. 2.3. Its main computing platform is a pair of HP servers, each with two quad-core processors.

In the perception module, there are three submodules: object classification, localization, and road detection. Here, object classification first detects obstacles and then classifies them as either static or dynamic. The localization submodule yields the vehicle position and direction in the 3D world. The road detection submodule extracts a road coverage map and lane position.

The planning module uses a Hybrid Deliberative-Reactive model, which consists of upper level decisions and lower level reactions as separate components. The

[1] http://cs.stanford.edu/group/roadrunner/.

[2] http://www.me.vt.edu/urbanchallenge/.

**Fig. 2.3** The intelligent vehicle Odin developed by the Team VictorTango (published courtesy of Virginia Polytechnic Institute and State University)

coarsest level of planning is the route planner responsible for road segments and zones the vehicle should travel in. The driving behavior component takes care of obeying road rules. Motion planning is in charge of translating control commands into actuator control signals.

## 2.5 Massachusetts Institute of Technology—Talos

Team MIT has developed an urban autonomous vehicle, called Talos[3] (shown in Fig. 2.4) [1, 9, 13]. There are three key novel features: (i) perception-based navigation strategy; (ii) a unified planning and control architecture; (iii) a powerful new software infrastructure. Moreover, this vehicle consists of various submodules: Road Paint Detector, Navigator, Lane Tracker, Driveability Map, Obstacle Detector, Motion Planner, Fast Vehicle Detector, Controller, Positioning Modules. The perception module includes obstacle detector, hazard detector and lane tracking submodules. Planning a control algorithm involves using a navigator, driveability map, motion planner, and a controller. The navigator plays an important role in mission-level behavior, and the rest of these submodules work together in a tight coupling to yield the desired motion control goal in complex driving conditions.

[3] http://grandchallenge.mit.edu/.

**Fig. 2.4** The intelligent vehicle Talos developed by the Team MIT (published courtesy of Massachusetts Institute of Technology)

**Fig. 2.5** The intelligent vehicle Skynet developed by Team Cornell (published courtesy of Cornell University)

## 2.6 Cornell University—Skynet

Team Cornell's Skynet[4] is a modified Chevrolet Tahoe, shown in Fig. 2.5, and consists of two groups of sensors [15]. One group is used for sensing vehicle itself, and the other group (laser, radar and vision) is for sensing the environment. Thanks to the above sensors, Skynet is capable of providing real-time position, velocity, and

[4]http://www.cornellracing.com/.

attitude for absolute positioning. Moreover, Skynet's local map including obstacle detection information is the map of local environment surrounding Skynet. In many cases, autonomous driving in complex scenes is more than basic obstacle avoidance. Hence, the vehicle-centric local map is not enough for absolute positioning. We need to estimate environment structures using posterior pose and track generator algorithms.

Skynet is using the probabilistic representation of the environment to plan mission paths within the context of the rule-based road network. One intelligent planner includes three primary layers: a behavioral layer, a tactical layer, and a operational layer. The goal of the behavior layer is to determine the fastest route to the next mission point. When there exist state transitions in the behavior layer, the corresponding component of the tactical layer is executed. Among the four tactical components, the road tactical component is to seek a proper lane and to monitor other agents in the same and neighboring lanes. The intersection tactical component handles intersection queuing behavior and safe merging. The zone tactical component takes care of basic navigation in unconstrained cases. The blockage tactical component implements obstacle detection and judging whether there are temporary traffic jams, and acts accordingly. The final layer is an operational layer which is in charge of converting local driving boundaries and a reference speed into actuators, steering wheels, throttles, and brakes.

## 2.7 University of Pennsylvania and Lehigh University—Little Ben

Little Ben[5] designed by the Ben Franklin Racing Team is a modified Toyota Prius with various sensors and computers for the 2007 DARPA Urban Challenge [4], shown in Fig. 2.6. Similar to other intelligent vehicles, Little Ben is equipped with various sensors, such as three LMS291, two SICK LDRS, and a Bumble bee stereo camera. The sensor array provides timely information about the surrounding environment, which is integrated into a dynamic map for environment perception and modeling.

Little Ben's software framework consists of perception, planning, and control. Its perception module is responsible for providing static obstacles, moving vehicles, lane markings, and traversable ground. Little Ben's primary medium-to-long-range lidars are responsible for geometric obstacles and ground classification, road making extraction, and dynamic obstacle tracking. Moreover, the stereo vision system is used to detect close road makings. Once the perception module generates information about static obstacles, dynamic obstacles, and lane markings, the MapPlan module will update obstacles and lane marking likelihoods in a map centered at the current vehicle location. The mission and path planning consists of two stages. The first stage is to calculate the optional path by minimizing the mission time. The next

---

[5] http://benfranklinracingteam.org/.

**Fig. 2.6** The intelligent vehicle Little Ben (published courtesy of the University of Pennsylvania and Lehigh University)

stage is to incorporate the dynamic map into new path planning. Afterwards, the path follower module is responsible for calculating the vehicle steering and throttle-brake commands to follow the desired trajectory.

## 2.8 Oshkosh Truck Corporation—TerraMax

The TerraMax Vehicle[6] is a joint effort by Oshkosh Truck Corp., Rockwell Collins, and the University of Parma [5], and is shown in Fig. 2.7. In this vehicle, Rockwell Collins was in charge of the intelligent vehicle management system. Oshkosh Truck Corporation was working on project organization, system integration, low level control hardware, modeling and simulation support, and the vehicle, while the University of Parma provided the vision module. The most important feature is that this vehicle has big size (weighs around 30000 pounds, is 27 feet long, 8 feet wide, and 8 feet high), so it has to travel slowly.

Considering dynamic analysis of its mechanical systems, TerraMax provides underbody, steer angles, and lateral stability information for control modules. The full vehicle model consists of suspensions, steering, chassis, and tires. A typical simulation method over 70 different obstacles is used to evaluate the underbody clearance, for better handling of different obstacles at low speeds. The steering simulation is used to allocate both the front and rear steering angles, when given a steering wheel input. In addition, constant-radius tests were used to evaluate the lateral stability of the truck.

The intelligent Vehicle Management system (iVMS) developed by the Rockwell Collins is an interface between the vehicle systems and onboard sensors. Moreover,

[6]http://en.wikipedia.org/wiki/TerraMax_(vehicle).

**Fig. 2.7** The intelligent vehicle TerraMax (published courtesy of the Oshkosh Truck Corporation)

the iVMS provides various autonomous functions, such as vehicle control, real time path planning, obstacle detection, behavior management, and navigation.

## References


1. Aoude, G.S., How, J.P.: Using support vector machines and Bayesian filtering for classifying agent intentions at road intersections. The Association for Computational Linguistics (2009)
2. Bacha, A., Bauman, C., Faruque, R., Fleming, M., Terwelp, C., Reinholtz, C., Hong, D., Wicks, A., Alberi, T., Anderson, D., et al.: Odin: team victortango's entry in the DARPA urban challenge. J. Field Robot. **25**(8), 467–492 (2008)
3. Bishop, R.: A survey of intelligent vehicle applications worldwide. In: Proceedings of the IEEE on Intelligent Vehicles Symposium, 2000. IV 2000, pp. 25–30. IEEE, New York (2000)
4. Bohren, J., Foote, T., Keller, J., Kushleyev, A., Lee, D., Stewart, A., Vernaza, P., Derenick, J., Spletzer, J., Satterfield, B.: Little Ben: The Ben Franklin racing teams entry in the 2007 DARPA Urban Challenge. DARPA Urban Challenge **25**(9), 231–255 (2009)
5. Braid, D., Broggi, A., Schmiedel, G.: The TerraMax autonomous vehicle. J. Field Robot. **23**(9), 693–708 (2006)
6. Crisman, J.D., Thorpe, C.E.: UNSCARF—a color vision system for the detection of unstructured roads. In: Proc. of the IEEE International Conference on Robotics and Automation (1991)
7. Crisman, J.D., Thorpe, C.E.: SCARF: a color vision system that tracks roads and intersections. IEEE Trans. Robot. Autom. **9**(1), 49–58 (1993)
8. Herbert, M.H., Thorpe, C., Stentz, A.: Intelligent Unmanned Ground Vehicles: Autonomous Navigation Research at Carnegie Mellon. Kluwer Academic, Norwell (1997)
9. Huang, A.S., Antone, M., Olson, E., Fletcher, L., Moore, D., Teller, S., Leonard, J.: A high-rate, heterogeneous data set from the DARPA Urban Challenge. Int. J. Robot. Res. **29**(13), 1595 (2010)

10. Iagnemma, K., Buehler, M.: Editorial for journal of field robotics special issue on the DARPA grand challenge. J. Field Robot. **23**(9), 655–656 (2006)
11. Jochem, T.M., Pomerleau, D.A., Thorpe, C.E.: MANIAC: a next generation neurally based autonomous road follower. In: Proceedings of the International Conference on Intelligent Autonomous Systems: IAS-3, Pittsburgh, Pennsylvania, USA (1993)
12. Kluge, K., Thorpe, C.: Intersection detection in the YARF road following system. In: Intelligent Autonomous Systems, IAS–3: An International Conference, Pittsburgh, Pennsylvania. IOS Press, Amsterdam (1993)
13. Leonard, J., How, J., Teller, S., Berger, M., Campbell, S., Fiore, G., Fletcher, L., Frazzoli, E., Huang, A., Karaman, S., et al.: A perception-driven autonomous urban vehicle. DARPA Urban Challenge **25**(10), 163–230 (2009)
14. Montemerlo, M., Becker, J., Bhat, S., Dahlkamp, H., Dolgov, D., Ettinger, S., Haehnel, D., Hilden, T., Hoffmann, G., Huhnke, B., et al.: Junior: the Stanford entry in the urban challenge. J. Field Robot. **25**(9), 569–597 (2008)
15. Pisoni, A.: Skynet. Manual version 0.9, http://skynet.rubyforge.org/, **3** (2007)
16. Pomerleau, D.A.: Neural network based autonomous navigation. In: Vision and Navigation. The Carnegie Mellon Navlab, pp. 83–93 (1990)
17. Thorpe, C., Hebert, M.H., Kanade, T., Shafer, S.A.: Vision and navigation for the Carnegie–Mellon Navlab. IEEE Trans. Pattern Anal. Mach. Intell. **10**(3), 362–373 (1988)
18. Urmson, C., Anhalt, J., Bagnell, D., Baker, C., Bittner, R., Clark, M., Dolan, J., Duggins, D., Galatali, T., Geyer, C., et al.: Autonomous driving in urban environments: boss and the urban challenge. J. Field Robot. **25**(8), 425–466 (2008)

# Chapter 3
# The Framework of Intelligent Vehicles

## 3.1 Introduction

The Asian Development Bank states: "In the five years 2000–2004, more than 500,000 people were killed and around 2.6 million injured in road accidents in the People's Republic of China (PRC), equivalent to one death every 5 minutes—the highest rate in the world." and estimates a yearly economic loss of $12.5 billion. Driver assistance and safety warning systems promise to provide partial solutions to these problems, and consequently many research efforts [1] aim at developing algorithms and building frameworks for them.

Road situation analysis requires not only obstacle information at the current time, but also predicted obstacle information at a future time. Indeed, an experienced driver looks several seconds along the road and bases his actions on information so obtained. This previewing of the road is necessary to avoid accidents since vehicle dynamics limits the car in making speed or direction changes.

$I^2$DASW uses more than one kind of sensors: image sensors, lidar, and radar. No single sensor can provide input as complete, robust, and accurate as required by $I^2$DASW. Image sensors have some problems, such as low ability of sensing depth, higher computation burden than lidar and radar. Radar shows limited lateral spatial information because either it is not available at all, or the field of view is narrow, or the resolution is reduced at large distances. Although lidar has a wide view field solving part of the previous problems, there are other problems, such as low ability of discrimination, clustering error, and recognition latency. These restrictions of the different sensor types explain the attention given to sensor fusion in research on object detection and tracking [1, 3], resulting a wide spectrum of promising applications in assistance driving, including multi-sensor Adaptive Cruise Control (ACC), fusion of advanced ACC and lane keeping systems [5], and smart airbag systems.

On the basis of the work [15, 16], we proposed a road safety situation and threat analysis algorithm and framework based on driver behavior and vehicle dynamics. In a current environment modeling phase, obstacles are detected and tracked by fusing various sensors depending on applications. In a future situation assessment, we use the position and size information of obstacles at the current time and vehicle

H. Cheng, *Autonomous Intelligent Vehicles*,
Advances in Computer Vision and Pattern Recognition,
DOI 10.1007/978-1-4471-2280-7_3, © Springer-Verlag London Limited 2011

dynamics equation to predict the future road situation at the time $k+1$. For lidar data, we distinguish the object types: static or moving objects, by estimating object speed.

The remainder of this chapter as follows. Section 3.2 introduces the state-of-the-art related to road safety frameworks. In Sect. 3.3, we provide a detailed description of our interactive safety analysis framework.

## 3.2 Related Work

Road situation analysis for driver assistance and safety warning is an interdisciplinary endeavor involving a lot of research fields, for instance, computer science, automobile engineering, cognitive science, and psychology, etc. It involves not only looking-in but also looking-out of a vehicle [12]. We classify these frameworks analyzing obstacle situation in a traffic scene into two categories. The first one is a current situation analysis framework which attempts to provide the vehicle and the driver with the obstacles' state in the current time. Generally, sensor fusion is used to estimate the current obstacles' state [3, 4, 13]. The other one is obstacle situation prediction in the future [2]. To assess the future situation, many prediction approaches have been used, such as the Extended Kalman Filter (EKF), Monte Carlo method [2], and Bayesian network [10].

Real-time safety analysis in traffic involving driver, vehicle, traffic environment, and their interaction is a challenge for perception, modeling, and control. Several safety analysis frameworks have been proposed to address different aspects in a road situation [2, 4, 6, 12]. In [2], a Monte Carlo reasoning framework is to evaluate the probability of a future collision and use a Monte Carlo importance sampling for the approximation of a collision integral. The looking-in and looking-out framework proposed by M.M. Trivedi et al. is a system-oriented safer driving framework [12] which consists of driving ecology sensing, hierarchical context processing, and modeling of drivers, vehicles, and environment. They build the Human-Centered Intelligent Driving Support System (HC-IDSS) to emphasize the role of driver. In context of an earthwork vehicle, a distributed sensor network aims at processing data acquired by different sensors, integrating them, and producing an interpretation of the environment observed [4], its main objectives of low-level and high-level data fusion are to obtain a rough and an accurate estimate of the number of objects present in the observed scene and their 3D positions, respectively. In addition, intersection scenario analysis was done in the INTERSAFE project, showing the need of driver assistance systems for intersection safety [6], where two parallel approaches, Top–Down-Approach and Down–Top-Approach, were realized. In these approaches, a dynamic risk assessment is done based on object tracking and classification, and the intent of a driver. Consequently, potential conflicts with other road users can be reported only a few seconds in advance.

This chapter proposes an integrated current and future safety situation analysis framework as general as possible, where we model not only the sensing phase, but also the control phase. In this framework, a speed estimation algorithm based on

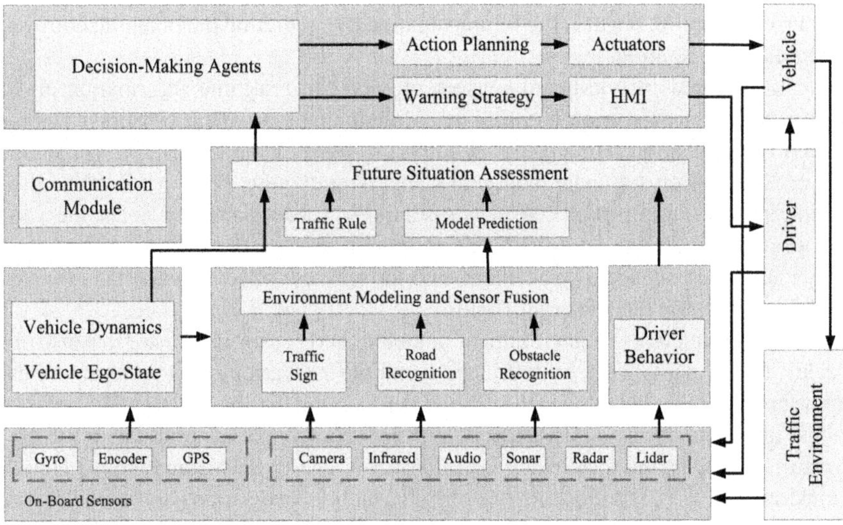


**Fig. 3.1** Interactive road situation analysis framework

lidar data is used to distinguish two types of obstacles: static objects and moving objects. On the basis of the speed and type of obstacles, we form obstacle tracks only using a single sensor, and following that a track fusion approach is used to yield accurate and robust global tracks. We use camera to detect lanes and obstacles in a Regions of Interest (ROIs) generated by range sensors, such as vehicles and pedestrians. Combining the lane structure with obstacle tracks, we can model the traffic environment and assess road situation at both the current and a near future time. We will introduce multiple-sensor based multiple-object detection and tracking module in Chap. 6.

## 3.3 Interactive Safety Analysis Framework

Many existing robotics technologies apply to intelligent assistance driving [14], however, much research work neglects the preview of a driver and driver response delay; moreover, the behavior of high speed vehicles differs greatly from other robots. For safe driving, a driver is in the center of the safety analysis [12], driver response delay together with other factors restricts the driving path of a vehicle. On the basis of these factors, we proposed an integrated interactive road safety analysis framework, where the system consists of the following modules: on-board sensor network, environment modeling and sensor fusion, vehicle ego-state and vehicle dynamics module, future situation assessment, decision-making agents, Human–Machine Interface (HMI), and a preview-following model based control module (see Fig. 3.1). In this framework, we consider a driver assistance system as a vehicle–driver–environment interactive closed-loop system; moreover, we focus on not only the current situation but also the future situation by predicting the potential collision probability distribution.

In our framework, on-board sensors provide the real-time information about drivers, traffic environment, and vehicles. How to configure these sensors is closely related to application domain. For example, in light of the requirement of multi-sensor ACC systems, maybe radar and camera are enough, but for pedestrian protection systems, an infrared sensor is essential to robust detection under the various weather conditions. In general, the external sensors capture object appearance, range, and voice outside a vehicle, and interior sensors collect vehicle state, such as speed, acceleration, and steering angle.

The main functions of environment modeling and sensor fusion are to sense obstacles, to recognize lane and traffic sign, and to fuse various sensors to model the environment. Lane detection is the problem of locating lane boundaries. We propose robust lane boundaries on a variety of different road types under a variety of illumination changes and shadowing by introducing an adaptive Randomized Hough Transform (RHT) [11]. For moving objects, such as pedestrians and vehicles, we use statistical background modeling techniques for the detection of such moving objects. For instance, we obtain the dynamic background model under the conditions of no passing vehicle and update the model when a passing vehicle enter into the field of view for the close cut-in and overtaking vehicle detection.

At the situation assessment level, road safety situation in the future is assessed by combining traffic rules, vehicle dynamics, and environment prediction. Since the safety distance varies with the speed of a host vehicle, we adopt preview time rather than safety distance as the measurement of safety response. Hence, the safety response time is given by

$$T_o = \frac{d_r + d_v + d_s}{v}, \tag{3.1}$$

where $d_r$ is the distance required to respond to the nearest object due to driver response delay, $d_v$ is the distance to slow down, $d_s$ is the safety distance between the host vehicle and obstacles, and $v$ is the velocity of the host vehicle.

Decision-making agents have two functions, one is to generate warning strategies for warning systems, such as route guide systems and the warning display device; the other is to make decisions about the expected path of action planning interfacing with actuators. A Preview Optimal Curvature (POC) model based on the Preview and Following Model (PFM) and driver behavior characteristic is utilized to control vehicle's velocity and direction, where the key problem is to establish fuzzy evaluation indexes and their membership functions that represent the front road geometry shape, traffic rules and driver behavior. For the details we refer to [7]. Here decision-making agents use the rigid kinematics and vehicle dynamics stable-state response properties to yield expected path, and then action planning updates the ideal path by using vehicle dynamics dynamic-state response properties. Their main interaction activities involve a driver operating a vehicle and a vehicle producing the lateral and longitudinal motion.

Furthermore, this framework involves communication and HMI modules. Communication modules implement information sharing between vehicles and between a vehicle and a base station. An HMI module present warning information from the decision and path planning module to the driver. The interaction between the vehicle and traffic environment mainly focuses on vehicle–vehicle communication and vehicle–base station communication. Vehicles in the future will be able to share the information about the environment to provide cooperative, convenient and safer driving.

On the basis of the Preview–Follow theory proposed by [8, 9], we proposed a region-based Preview–Follow

$$J(t) = \int_{t_1}^{t_2} \left[ y_e(S, t+\xi) - y_r(S, t+\xi) \right]^2 p(S, \xi)\, d\xi, \tag{3.2}$$

where $p(S, \xi)$ is the prior probability distribution given the region $S$ and the time increment $\xi$; $y_e(S, t)$ and $y_r(S, t)$ are the expected and the real drivable region at the time $t$, respectively; $\xi$ is the time increment. For the curve-based preview model, (3.2) simplifies to

$$J(t) = \int_{t_1}^{t_2} \left[ y_e(t+\xi) - y_r(t+\xi) \right]^2 p(\xi)\, d\xi, \tag{3.3}$$

where $y_e(t)$ and $y_r(t)$ are the expected and the real path at the time $t$, respectively.

Considering the fixed curvature, we assume that the ideal path of a vehicle is

$$y_r^*(t+\xi) = y_r(t) + \xi \dot{y}_r(t) + \frac{\xi^2}{2} \ddot{y}(t). \tag{3.4}$$

For the optimum curvature control, we write the vehicle acceleration as

$$\ddot{y}_r(t) = \left[ y_e'(t) - y_r(t) \int_{t_1}^{t_2} \xi^2 p(\xi)\, d\xi - c_1 \dot{y}_r(t) \right] / c_2, \tag{3.5}$$

where

$$c_1 = \int_{t_1}^{t_2} \xi^3 p(\xi)\, d\xi, \tag{3.6}$$

$$c_2 = \int_{t_1}^{t_2} \frac{\xi^4}{4} p(\xi)\, d\xi, \tag{3.7}$$

$$y_e'(t) = \int_{t_1}^{t_2} \xi^2 p(\xi) y_e(t+\xi)\, d\xi. \tag{3.8}$$

On the basis of the factors of road safety reasoning [2], we extend the factors of the future road situation given below.

1. *Traffic rules* While a driver implements a driving activity, traffic rules have a potential effect on the expected path. Traffic rules on highways and urban roads ensure safe, comfortable, collision-free driving. To achieve these objectives, the driver and the on-board sensors must recognize the traffic signs.
2. *Vehicle dynamics* The motion of a vehicle is restricted by vehicle dynamics and includes two factors: the internal factor involving the tires, steering systems, and acceleration/deceleration systems and the other external factor involving driver

instruction. In our framework, we consider it as a whole to affect the safe driving rather than look at each influencing sub-factor, and focus on vehicle stable-state and dynamic-state response properties.

3. *Driver behavior* The aim of $I^2$DASW systems is to develop an automatic system that can fully or partly replace a professional and experienced driver. Clearly, driver behavior characteristic are inevitably involved in safe driving. Except for road conditions and vehicle mechanical failures, most of traffic accidents are caused by drivers, for instance, inappropriate speed, ignoring right of way, overtaking, following too close, etc. In real-life traffic scenes, driving behavior, such as driver response delay, deeply affects the driving operation.
4. *Sensor uncertainty* Sensor noise causes uncertainty in data. The incomplete information is used to assess the scene, and modeling the background and dynamic object is a challenge given the incomplete and uncertain information.
5. *Vehicle state* Vehicle state includes position, velocity, acceleration, direction angle, yaw angle, etc. Yaw angle affects greatly the dynamic properties of a vehicle. Given the basic state parameters, we can generate a predicted path.

$I^2$DASW systems have three major functions:

1. Providing appropriate just-in-time information about the vehicle, driver, and traffic environment for safer and better driving. For example, Real-Time Traffic and Traveler Information (RTTI) aims at facilitating the access to public data and providing drivers with information about the traffic environment and the other vehicles.
2. Safety warning and assistance systems. The system warns the driver proactively about a possible hazardous situation on the basis of the vehicle's current position, orientation, and speed, and the road situation; moreover, steps can be taken to control the vehicle when a person's vehicle is in a hazardous situation. The safety warning systems monitor the driving situation and provide the traffic situation for drivers, for example, potential collision information, including route guide systems, Lane Change Decision Aid Systems (LCDAS), Traffic Impediment Warning Systems (TIWS), Forward Vehicle Collision Warning Systems (FVCWS), etc. Safety assistance systems use the warning information to generate the expected path and control the vehicle directly. Typical systems are Forward Collision Avoidance Assistance Systems (FCAAS), ACC systems, Low Speed Following Systems (LSFS), Stop & Go systems, etc.
3. In-vehicle safety protection device for drivers and passengers. Such a system can protect drivers and passengers from the impact between humans and vehicle bodies, for example, smart airbag systems.

## References

1. Afreixo, V., Ferreira, P.J.S.G., Santos, D.: Fourier analysis of symbolic data: a brief review. Digit. Signal Process. **14**(6), 523–530 (2004)
2. Broadhurst, A., Baker, S., Kanade, T.: Monte Carlo road safety reasoning. In: Proc. of the IEEE Intelligent Vehicles Symposium, pp. 319–324 (2005)

3. Escamilla-Ambrosio, P., Lieven, N.: A multiple-sensor multiple-target tracking approach for the autotaxi system. In: Proc. of the IEEE Intelligent Vehicles Symposium, pp. 601–606 (2004)
4. Foresti, G.L., Regazzoni, C.S.: Multisensor data fusion for autonomous vehicle navigation in risky environments. IEEE Trans. Vehicle Technol. **51**(5), 1165–1185 (2002)
5. Fritz, H., Gern, A., Schiemenz, H., Bonnet, C.: CHAUFFEUR assistant: a driver assistance system for commercial vehicles based on fusion of advanced ACC and lane keeping. In: The IEEE Intelligent Vehicles Symposium, pp. 495–500 (2004). IEEE, New York
6. Fuerstenberg, K., Rössler, B.: A new European approach for intersection safety—the EC-Project INTERSAFE. In: Proc. of the IEEE Intelligent Transportation Systems Conference, pp. 493–504 (2005)
7. Gao, Z., Zheng, N., Guan, H., Guo, K.: Application of driver direction control model in intelligent vehicle's decision and control algorithm. In: IEEE Transaction on Intelligent Transportation Systems, vol. 2, pp. 413–418 (2002)
8. Guo, K.H.: Preview-follower method for closed-loop system directional control. In: 19'th America Anua Conference on Human Machine (1983)
9. Guo, K.H.: Vehicle Operational Dynamics. JiLin Press of Science and Technology, China (1991)
10. Kawasaki, N., Kiencke, U.: Standard platform for sensor fusion on advanced driver assistance system using Bayesian network. In: Proc. of the IEEE Intelligent Vehicles Symposium, pp. 250–255 (2004)
11. Li, Q., Zheng, N., Cheng, H.: Springrobot: a prototype autonomous vehicle and its algorithms for lane detection. IEEE Trans. Intell. Transp. Syst. **5**(4), 300–308 (2004)
12. McCall, J.C., Achler, O., Trivedi, M.M., Haué, J.B., Fastrez, P., Forster, D., Hollan, J.D., Boer, E.: A collaborative approach for human-centered driver assistance systems. In: Proc. of the IEEE Intelligent Transportation Systems Conference, pp. 663–667 (2004)
13. Mobus, R., Kolbe, U.: Multi-target multi-object tracking, sensor fusion of radar and infrared. In: Proc. of the IEEE Intelligent Vehicles Symposium, pp. 732–737 (2004)
14. Urmson, C.: The robotics institute. In: Navigation Regimes for Off-Road Autonomy (2005)
15. Zhang, X.T.: Interactive road safety analysis and warning systems. Master Thesis, Xi'an Jiaotong University (2006)
16. Zheng, N.N., Tang, S., Cheng, H., Li, Q., Lai, G., Wang, F.W.: Toward intelligent driver-assistance and safety warning system. IEEE Intell. Syst. **19**(2), 8–11 (2004)

# Part II
# Environment Perception and Modeling

# Chapter 4
# Road Detection and Tracking

## 4.1 Introduction

Road detection and tracking are important tasks for many intelligent vehicle applications, such as Lane Departure Warning (LDW) systems, Anti-sleep systems,[1] driver assistance and safety warning systems [49], autonomous driving [9]. Road detection means locating road boundaries without the prior knowledge of road geometry, and includes a few basic tasks, namely, road localization, calculating the position of a vehicle with respect to the road, while road tracking is to update the road parameters from previous road parameters. Video-based road detection and tracking keep drawing more and more attention to this subject since it has many advantages compared to active sensors. In general, there are two types of road detection and tracking approaches: one is for structured roads with yellow or white lane markings, the other is for unstructured roads.

The main advantages of video-based approach are as follows:

- Vision sensors acquire data in a non-invasive way, thus not polluting the road environment. In other words, vision sensors do not interfere with each other when multiple intelligent vehicles are moving within the same area. By contrast, besides the problem of environment pollution, we have to carefully think about some typical problems of active sensors, such as the wide variation in reflection ratios caused by different reasons (such as obstacles shape or material), the need for the maximum signal level to comply with some safety rules, and the interference among active sensors of the same type.
- In most of Intelligent Transportation Systems (ITS) and Intelligent Vehicle (IV) applications, vision sensors play a fundamental role, for example, in lane marking localization, traffic sign recognition, obstacle recognition. Among those applications, other sensors, such as laser and radar, are only complementary to vision sensors.
- We do not need to modify road infrastructures when using vision sensors to capture visual information. This is extremely important in practice applications.

---

[1] http://www.smarteye.se.

H. Cheng, *Autonomous Intelligent Vehicles*,
Advances in Computer Vision and Pattern Recognition,
DOI 10.1007/978-1-4471-2280-7_4, © Springer-Verlag London Limited 2011

- Vision sensors can get visual information with high spatial and temporal resolution about road environment. Whereas both radar and laser sensors have the same problems of low spatial and temporal resolutions.

Hence, vision sensors possess key advantages over active ones, for foreseeing in massive and widespread applications on autonomous intelligent vehicles. At the same time, vision-based road detection and tracking approaches have a few limitations:

- Vision sensors are less robust than laser sensors and radar sensors in extreme illumination conditions, such as fog, night, sunshine, rain.
- Large amount of video/image data is a great challenge for embedded systems. As a result, specific computer architectures and parallel processing techniques are carefully considered to improve real-time performance.
- On a bright sunny day, various objects, such as trees, buildings, cars, bridges, and channels, could generate shadows, thus changing road color and textures.
- On-road vehicles and obstacles could occlude part of a road, thus resulting in discontinuity of lane markings.

In addition, to improve road detection and speed up the processing, some assumptions in road detection and tracking are made:

- High contrast between lane markings and other part constraints: Apparently, the lane markings are highly contrasted by road backgrounds, which is the basic assumption for almost all lane markings based approaches. Here, different color spaces are used in these approaches. Southall et al. extract lane markings from the red channel of color images since lane markings are either yellow or white [43]. Li et al. proposed to transform the RGB color space into $I_1 I_2 I_3$ color space [29], and the $I_2 = (R - B)/2$ component is normalized to form a gray image, called the $I_2$ image. The advantages of this transform are twofold: First, the high correlation among the R, G, and B components is removed. Second, the new color space is more effective with respect to the quality of segmentation and the computational complexity.
- The continuity of lane boundary and marking edges: The continuity of lane boundary and marking edges is another basic assumption. Though some lane markings are dashed, they are certainly continuous locally and could be linked to get a complete one.
- Regions of Interest (ROI) assumptions: Instead of processing the whole image, lane detection and tracking algorithms focus on specific regions of interest only. In a current image frame, lane detection and tracking algorithms will seek ROIs using the results of previously processed frames or assuming prior knowledge on the road environment. In the lane detection integrated with lane tracking, the current lane parameters are predicted using the parameters of the previous frame and the vehicle dynamics, thus yielding search regions for the current detection [36].
- The fixed lane width assumption: The assumption of a fixed or smoothly varying lane width allows enhancing the search criterion, thus limiting the search to

almost parallel lane markings. Furthermore, a lane marking feature extractor is based on the fact that lane marking width is in a small range of possible values on a road [25], which implies geometric constraints on the observed lane-marking width.

- Road geometric assumptions: The reconstruction of road geometry can be simplified by assuming its shape. In general, different models could correspond to different applications; we have to consider carefully. The commonly-used road models are straight road models [46], curved road models (Clothoid lane models [31, 43], parabola models [33], quadratic models [24]), 3D road models with horizontal and vertical curvature [26].

## 4.2 Related Work

In this section, we will introduce the state-of-the-art of road detection and tracking.

### *4.2.1 Model-Based Approaches*

Kluge et al. proposed a deformable template model of lane structures to locate lane boundaries without thresholding the intensity gradient information [37]. The Metropolis algorithm is used to maximize a function which evaluates how well the image gradient data supports a given set of template deformation parameters. Wang et al. presented a B-Snake which is capable to describe a wider range of lane structures and is constructed by a set of control points [45]. Moreover, Minimum Mean Square Error (MMSE) is used to estimate the control points by the overall image forces on two lanes. Tie Liu et al. presented lane detection algorithm using a deformable template and a Genetic Algorithm (GA) [30]. In this approach, the first step is to preprocess a road image using an edge operator to yield edges, and then fit a deformable template model of road edges or marked lines. Here, its likelihood function defines the fitting degree for a given template deformation parameters. Afterwards a GA is used to search the global optimal solution of the likelihood function, thus yielding the optimal parameters of the deformable road model.

### *4.2.2 Multi-cue Fusion Based Approach*

Apostoloff et al. proposed using particle filtering and multi-cue fusion technologies to robustly handle several lane detection and tracking issues, such as shadows on the road, unreliable lane markings, dramatic lighting changes, and discontinuous changes in road shapes and types [1]. Here, six cues are used in lane detection and tracking: lane markers, road edges, road colors, non-road colors, road width, and elastic lanes. Gern et al. presented a new approach fusing two different types of road features, white lane markings and horizontal optical flow [21]. First of all, a clothoidal lane geometrical approach is used to locally track the white markings. Second, inspired by human behavior when a driver is under adverse weather conditions, the horizontal optical flow is calculated to track the motion of all road parallel structures. As a result, this leads to a precise road position estimation and vehicle position relative to lanes, even under adverse weather conditions.

### 4.2.3 Hypothesis-Validation Based Approaches

Pomerleau et al. proposed determining the curvature of the road ahead using a 'Hypothesize and Validate' strategy [40]. The RALPH first hypothesizes road models with different curvatures, then subtracts these curvatures from the low-resolution image, and finally validates which hypothesized curvature matches well the original image.

### 4.2.4 Neural Network Based Approaches

In most prototypes of autonomous vehicles developed worldwide, road recognition and vehicle driving are two separate modules. However, some early systems were not based on the preliminary road detection, but obtained driving commands directly from road images. For example, Autonomous Land Vehicle in a Neural Net (ALVINN) is the Carnegie Mellon University's intelligent vehicle which consists of a single hidden layer back-propagation network [39]. Here, its input layer of NN is a $30 \times 32$ two-dimensional video frame and the output layer of NN is a linear representation of the travel directions of the vehicle so that the vehicle can be kept on the road. After training, the vehicle can autonomously follow the road. This system had driven on various road types under different conditions.

### 4.2.5 Stereo-Based Approaches

Stereo vision algorithms can relax the common assumptions about a road: flat road surfaces, constant pitch angles. Furthermore, depth information allows separating road from obstacles. S. Nedevschi et al. modeled lanes as a 3D surface, defined by the vertical and horizontal clothoid curves, the lane width, and the roll angle. Also, the lane detection is integrated into a tracking process. In addition, the Generic Obstacle and Lane Detection (GOLD) system is based on a stereo vision hardware and software architecture [4, 8, 35], where the Inverse Perspective Mapping (IPM) over both left and right stereo images is used to remove the perspective effect.

### 4.2.6 Temporal Correlation Based Approaches

When a road following algorithm is aimed at not only lane detection but also lane tracking, the temporal correlation between consecutive frames can be used either to ease the feature determination or to validate the result of the processing. Redmill et al. developed an image-based lane tracking system [41] in which the geometry and width of the current lane ahead of the vehicle are estimated frame by frame. Afterwards, the position and orientation of the vehicle are estimated w.r.t. the center line between the two lanes.

### 4.2.7 Image Filtering Based Approaches

McCall and Trivedi proposed a method for lane detection using steerable filters [32]. Steerable filters are robust with respect to lighting changes and shadows and work well in extracting both circular road markings as well as painted road markings. In addition, road/lane segmentation and obstacle detection in a dynamic scene as a part of the European PROMETHEUS project consist of a temporal filter, an edge detector, and a watershed transformation [6]. Here, the morphological 'watershed' transformation is used to locate the lane edges in the gradient images.

## 4.3 Lane Detection Using Adaptive Random Hough Transform

### 4.3.1 The Lane Shape Model

For structured road, lane models play an important role in lane detection, where some assumptions are made to better recovery 3D lanes from 2D images. In this section, we assume that the two lane marks are parallel lines and also concentric circular arcs on a flat ground plane. Let a pixel $(u, v)$ in an image plane correspond to a point $(x, y)$ on the ground plane. Hence, a circular arc with curvature $k$ is approximated by a parabola of the form

$$x = \frac{1}{2}ky^2 + my + b, \tag{4.1}$$

where $b$ is the offset of the arc on the ground plane. These circular arcs on the ground plane are projected into curves in the image plane. These curves can be closely approximated in the image plane by [28]

$$u = \frac{k'}{v - h_z} + b'(v - h_z) + u_0, \tag{4.2}$$

where $k' = \alpha k$; $b'$ is related to $b$, arc curvature $k'$, and the camera tilt angle; $u_0$ is a function of the tangent of the arc on the ground plane and the camera tilt.

Taking the derivative of (4.2), we have

$$b' = \frac{du}{dv} + \frac{k'}{(v - hz)^2}. \tag{4.3}$$

Then (4.2) can be represented by

$$u = \frac{2k}{v - h_z} + \frac{du}{dv}(v - h_z) + v_p. \tag{4.4}$$

Now we transform the 3D parametric space of $k', b', v_p$ into the 2D parametric space of $k', v_p$, thus reducing computational complexity and storage requirements. Furthermore, both $k'$ and $v_p$ are the same for all lane shape features, whereas $b'$ is feature specific. In other words, among these lane shape features, lane edges approximately share $k'$ and $v_p$. The difference between them is the value of the parameter $b$. This allows us to estimate $k'$ and $v_p$ robustly and quickly by Random Hough Transform (RHT). Therefore, both $k'$ and $v_p$ can be estimated directly from the raw edge point location and orientation without grouping the edge points together into individual features.

Given two pixels, $(u_1, v_1)$ and $(u_2, v_2)$, sampled in the gray-edge map, $k'$ and $v_p$ can be calculated as

$$\begin{cases} k' = \frac{1}{2}\frac{(u_1-u_2)-\frac{du}{dv}(v_1-v_2)}{(v_1-h_z)^{-1}-(v_2-h_z)^{-1}}, \\ v_p = u_1 - 2\frac{k'}{v_1-h_z} - \frac{du}{dv}(v_1 - h_z). \end{cases} \tag{4.5}$$

Finally, we formulate lane detection as estimating $k'$ and $b'$ for the left and the right lane in road images.

### 4.3.2 The Adaptive Random Hough Transform

Hough Transform (HT) is a classic parameter estimation approach, which is widely used in lane detection [17, 22, 34, 47]. Since image features can be used independently, the HT is suitable for implementing in a parallel computing system. Rallard et al. generalized the HT to detect arbitrary shapes under a geometric transform [3]. However, increasing the number, range, and accuracy of the parameters may result in high computing complexity. In line detection, Illingworth et al. proposed implementing the HT efficiently by an adaptive accumulator array and a coarse-to-fine strategy. The advantage of this approach is that it can yield a solution until a given accuracy without increasing array size. In addition, a two-step adaptive generalized HT for the detection of non-analytic objects under weak affine transformations was introduced in [16].

RHT can improve efficiency in the detection of an analytic curve edge map, determining the $n$ parameters of the curve of interest. By contrast, the RHT has higher

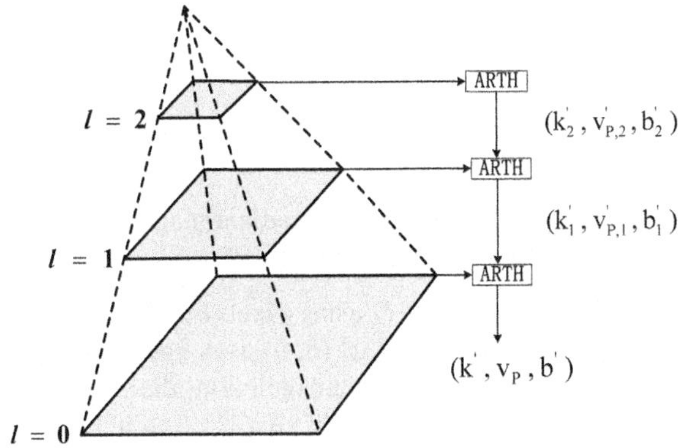


**Fig. 4.1** The ARTH algorithm flow

parameter accuracy, larger scope of the parameter space, smaller storage requirements, and higher speed. However, the procedure is repeated to combine the discrete parameter values. Thereby, the wide range and high accuracy of the parameters could yield remarkably large computing burden and storage space requirements.

Motivated by these problems, we present a new Adaptive RHT (ARHT) for lane detection, which combines the advantage of both the AHT and RHT. Figure 4.1 is the algorithm flow of the ARHT that illustrates the implementation strategy to detect the lane markings in a road image.

**A. Pixel Sampling on Edges** The task of lane detection can be conducted on a binary edge image usually from grey-level images by either simple thresholding operations or by some standard edge detection techniques.

However, when using gradient operator to obtain edges, it is difficult to determine an optimal threshold for selecting only true road lanes corresponding to the painted yellow and white lane marks or road boundaries among many noisy edges. Also, in many road scenes it is not possible to select a suitable threshold that eliminates noise edges without eliminating many of the lane edge points of interest. In lane detection, curves often disappear during the edge detection processes, and this becomes critical for the succeeding processes. Therefore, a better alternative is to use the whole gray edge map while no useful information is lost. However, computational cost is high if all pixels are included, a very low threshold value is assumed to insure the existence of true edges corresponding to road boundaries, and the remaining problem is the selection of the real boundaries among many candidate edges. For the gray edge magnitude map mentioned above, a very low threshold (e.g., 0.1 or 0.2) is set to remove those points which do not belong to lane markings, thus keeping low false negative rate.

In RHT based on a binary edge map, every edge pixel is sampled uniformly, without considering its probability of being on a certain curve. In the ARHT, inspired by particle filtering [2], pixels in the gray edge map are weighted according to its gradient magnitude, and then the pixels are sampled according to their weight, i.e., pixels with larger gradient magnitudes are sampled more frequently. Here, the weight of a pixel with index $n$ ($n = 0, 1, \ldots, N-1$) is defined as

$$w^{(n)}(u, v) = \frac{f_m^{(n)}(u, v)}{\sum_{u=0}^{W-1} \sum_{v=0}^{H-1} f_m^{(n-1)}(u, v)}, \tag{4.6}$$

where $f_m(u, v) = -\frac{du}{dv}$ is the gradient magnitude, and $\sum_{n=0}^{N-1} w^{(n)} = 1$.

The pixels are sampled as follows:

(a) Form a sample-set $D$ using pixels having nonzero gradient magnitude;
(b) Calculate the weight $w^n(u, v)$ as defined in (4.6).
(c) Store everything together including the cumulative probability as $(d^{(n)}, w^{(n)}, C^{(n)})$, where $C^{(0)} = 0$, $C^{(n)} = C^{(n-1)} + w^{(n)}$, $n = 0, 1, \ldots, N-1$.
(d) Generate a random number $r \in [0, 1]$.
(e) Find the smallest $q$ for which $C^{(q)} \geq r$ by binary subdivision.

We select $q$ elements of $D$ to be the sampled pixels. Afterwards, we estimate the parameters $k$ and $v_p$; the correctness of the parameters should also be verified. Since we cannot get lane shape from the parameters $k$ and $v_p$ only, parameter $b$ has to be calculated. The parameter $b$ of the model can be found by forming a histogram of the accumulation of gradient magnitude of points on the curve supposed to be true in the gray level edge image. The pixels throughout the curve can be accumulated as

$$M = \sum_{c \in Curve} f_m(u_c, v_c), \tag{4.7}$$

where $M$ represents the length of the curve determined by $k'$. If $M$ exceeds a specified threshold, the curve is true.

Once a marking is detected, the other marking can be obtained by some post analysis, such as a simple histogram step.

**B. Multi-Resolution Parameter Estimating Strategy** A multi-resolution strategy is used for both achieving a cumulative solution rapidly and reducing computing complexity. Now we build a Gaussian pyramid, where each level $I_l$ is smoothed by a symmetric Gaussian kernel and resampled to obtain the next level $I_{l+1}$ by [19]:

$$I_{l+1} = S_{\downarrow}(G_\sigma * I_l), \qquad I_0 = I, \tag{4.8}$$

where $I$ is the original image, $G_\sigma$ is a Gaussian kernel with bandwidth $\sigma$, $S_{\downarrow}(\cdot)$ is a downsampling operator. Figure 4.2 shows a multi-resolution image representation for lane detection.

Now we can roughly and efficiently locate the global optimum using the ARHT with a fixed accuracy. The parameters from the previous pyramid level are the initial parameters of the ARHT for estimating more accurate ones. By doing so, we constrain the parameter search to a smaller range around the previous solution, thus reducing computing complexity and storage space. This coarse-to-fine strategy offers us an acceptable solution at an affordable computational cost, and thus speeds up the lane detection.

**Fig. 4.2** Gaussian pyramid of road images with resolution from 256 × 240 to 64 × 60

In the Gaussian pyramid, the parameter relationships between the two consecutive pyramid levels are

$$k'_l = 4k'_{l+1}, \qquad v_{p,l} = 2v_{p,l+1}, \qquad b_l = b_l + 1. \tag{4.9}$$

Now, we discuss the error criterion regarding the elements in the ARHT. Usually, we consider two elements the same if they have the same coordinates. One alternative is that two elements are same if the distance between them is smaller than a given tolerance $\varepsilon$. The smaller the tolerance, the higher the parameter accuracy when using the ARHT. Although $\varepsilon$ is fixed in our approach, the parameter accuracy is still improved due to the multi-resolution image representation.

### 4.3.3 Experimental Results

This section presents the performance of the proposed method for the real road scenes. We can extract the left lane boundary and the right lane boundary. The algorithm is tested on some images from both the video grabbed by an on-board camera in our lab and the images provided by Robotics Institute of CMU.[2] All experimental images are 24-bit color images of size 256 × 240. Figure 4.3 shows some of our experimental results of lane boundary detection, where detected boundaries are superimposed onto the original images. These images represent various real highways scenes, including a lane whose left and right markings are solid, a lane whose left marking is solid and right marking is broken, a lane whose left marking is broken and right marking is solid, a lane whose left and right markings are broken, a lane with shadows, a lane with a highlight in the far field, a lane whose left marking has a big blank, also a lane whose markings are fragmentary. Experiment results show that the method retains the desirable HT characteristics of robustness to extraneous data and the ability to detect model parameters from disturbed data, although imperfect detection occasionally happens because of traffic signs drawn on the road.

[2] http://vasc.ri.cmu.edu/idb/html/road/index.html.

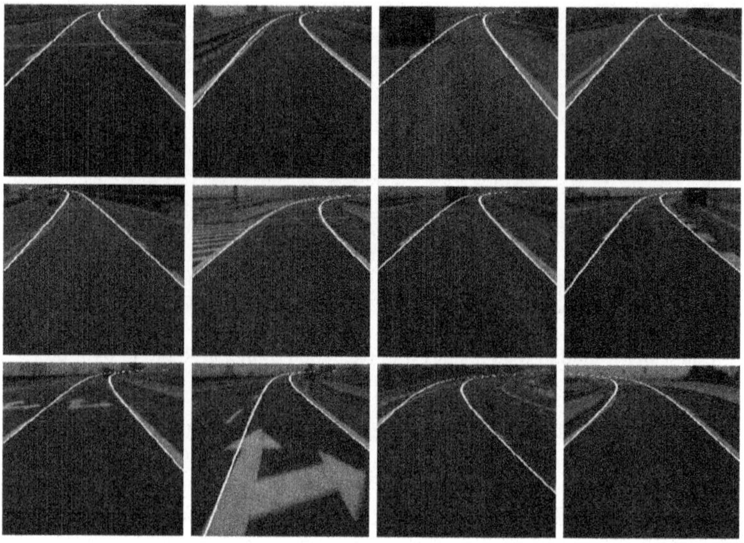

**Fig. 4.3** Experimental results on different road scenes

**Fig. 4.4** Experimental comparison of a genetic algorithm and the ARHT for lane detection

Figure 4.4 demonstrates the performance of genetic algorithm based lane detection [10] and ARHT based lane detection. The experimental comparison indicates that the latter has some advantages over the former.

## 4.4 Lane Tracking

### 4.4.1 Particle Filtering

In principle, particle filtering is a sequential Bayes filtering approach, a.k.a., sequential Monte Carlo filtering [15], which is widely used in lane tracking [38, 43]. Let $Z_k = \{z_0, z_1, \dots, z_k\}$ denote the measurement before time $k$, and $S_k = \{s_0, s_1, \dots, s_k\}$ denote the states before time $k$.

To better understand the particle filter, we briefly review Bayes' filtering. The Bayes' rule is

$$P(s|z) = \frac{P(z|s) \times P(s)}{P(z)} = \frac{\mathit{Likelihood} \times \mathit{Prior}}{\mathit{Evidence}}. \tag{4.10}$$

This equation indicates how we compute the posterior probability from the likelihood and the prior probability. In this Bayes' framework, we can determine $s$ by finding the most probable values of $s$ given data $z$. This technique is called Maximizing A Posterior (MAP). When $P(s)$ is a constant for any value of $s$, MAP can be simplified to a Maximum Likelihood Estimation (MLE).

Furthermore, the recursive Bayes' filtering consists of two steps: the prediction step and the updating step. In the prediction step, we calculate the value of $s$ at time $k$ according to a dynamic system model and a previous posterior probability at time $k-1$ by

$$p(s_k|Z_{k-1}) = \int p(s_k|s_{k-1}) p(s_{k-1}|Z_{k-1})\, ds_{k-1}, \tag{4.11}$$

where $p(s_k|s_{k-1})$ is a probability density function (*pdf*) of a dynamic model. Afterwards, the updating step calculates the $P(s_k|Z_k)$ given the likelihood and $p(s_k|Z_{k-1})$ by

$$P(s_k|Z_k) = \frac{P(z_k|s_k, Z_{k-1}) \times P(s_k|Z_{k-1})}{P(z_k|Z_{k-1})}, \tag{4.12}$$

where $P(z_k|s_k, Z_{k-1})$ is a measurement model, $P(s_k|Z_{k-1})$ is a prior model, and $P(z_k|Z_{k-1})$ is a constant and can be represented by

$$p(z_k|Z_{k-1}) = \int p(z_k|s_k) p(s_k|Z_{k-1})\, ds_k. \tag{4.13}$$

Now we turn to sampling algorithms to find the representation of the posterior probability. That is, we sample from the posterior distribution with some discrete and weighted particles the posterior distribution

$$\hat{p}(s_k|Z_k) = \frac{1}{N} \sum_{i=1}^{N} \delta\big(s_k - s_k^{(i)}\big), \tag{4.14}$$

where the $\{s_k^i\}_{i=1,\dots,N}$ are independent identically distributed (i.i.d.). Let $s_{0:k} = \{s_0, s_1, \dots, s_k\}$, and we can get any estimate of the form $f(s_{0:k})$ approximately by

$$E\left[f(s_{0:k})\right] = \int f(s_{0:k})p(s_{0:k}|Z_k)\,ds_{0:k} \approx \frac{1}{N}\sum_{i=1}^{N} f\left(s_{0:k}^{(i)}\right). \tag{4.15}$$

Unfortunately, it is often not possible to sample directly from the posterior distribution. Hence, we sample from a distribution $q(s_{0:k}|Z_k)$ which can be sampled easier, called the **Proposal Distribution**. Then we have

$$\begin{aligned} E\left[f(s_{0:k})\right] &= \int f(s_{0:k})\frac{p(s_{0:k}|Z_k)}{q(s_{0:k}|Z_k)}q(s_{0:k}|Z_k)\,ds_{0:k} \\ &= \int f(s_{0:k})\frac{p(Z_k|s_{0:k})p(s_{0:k})}{p(Z_k)q(s_{0:k}|Z_k)}q(s_{0:k}|Z_k)\,ds_{0:k}. \end{aligned} \tag{4.16}$$

Let $w_k(s_{0:k}) = \frac{p(Z_k|s_{0:k})p(s_{0:k})}{q(s_{0:k}|Z_k)}$. Since the probability $p(Z_k)$ is independent of $s_{0:k}$, the estimate can be expressed as follows:

$$\begin{aligned} E\left[f(s_{0:k})\right] &= \frac{1}{p(Z_k)}\int f(s_{0:k})w_k(s_{0:k})q(s_{0:k}|Z_k)\,ds_k \\ &= \frac{\int f(s_{0:k})w_k(s_{0:k})q(s_{0:k}|Z_k)\,ds_{0:k}}{\int p(Z_k|s_{0:k})p(s_{0:k})\frac{q(s_{0:k}|Z_k)}{q(s_{0:k}|Z_k)}\,ds_{0:k}} \\ &= \frac{\int f(s_{0:k})w_k(s_{0:k})q(s_{0:k}|Z_k)\,ds_{0:k}}{\int w_k(s_{0:k})q(s_{0:k}|Z_k)\,ds_{0:k}} \\ &= \frac{E_{q(s_{0:k}|Z_k)}[w_k(s_{0:k})f(s_{0:k})]}{E_{q(s_{0:k}|Z_k)}[w_k(s_{0:k})]}. \end{aligned} \tag{4.17}$$

Now we can estimate approximately by directly sampling from the proposal distribution $q(s_{0:k}|Z_k)$ and get

$$\begin{aligned} E\left[f(s_{0:k})\right] &\approx \frac{\frac{1}{N}\sum_{i=1}^{N} w_k(s_{0:k}^{(i)})f(s_{0:k}^{(i)})}{\frac{1}{N}\sum_{i=1}^{N} w_k(s_{0:k}^{(i)})} \\ &\approx \sum_{i=1}^{N} \widetilde{w}_k\left(s_{0:k}^{(i)}\right)f\left(s_{0:k}^{(i)}\right), \end{aligned} \tag{4.18}$$

where

$$\widetilde{w}_k\left(s_{0:k}^{(i)}\right) = \frac{w_k(s_{0:k}^{(i)})}{\sum_{j=1}^{N} w_k(s_{0:k}^{(j)})}. \tag{4.19}$$

The above procedure is called **Bayesian Importance Sampling**.

Since $q(s_{0:k}|Z_k) = q(s_k|s_{0:k-1}, Z_k)q(s_{0:k-1}|Z_{k-1})$, we have

$$\begin{aligned} w_k &= \frac{p(Z_k|s_{0:k})p(s_{0:k})}{q(s_{0:k}|Z_k)} = \frac{p(Z_k|s_{0:k})p(s_{0:k})}{q(s_{0:k}|Z_k, s_{0:k-1})q(s_{0:k-1}|Z_{k-1})} \\ &= \frac{p(Z_{k-1}|s_{0:k-1})p(s_{0:k-1})}{q(s_{0:k-1}|Z_{k-1})} \frac{p(Z_k|s_{0:k})}{p(Z_{k-1}|s_{0:k-1})} \frac{p(s_{0:k}}{p(s_{0:k-1})} \frac{1}{q(s_{0:k}|Z_k, s_{0:k-1})} \\ &= w_{k-1} \frac{p(z_k|s_k)p(s_k|s_{k-1})}{q(s_k|s_{k-1}, Z_k)}. \end{aligned} \tag{4.20}$$

Note that in the second row of (4.20), $p(z_k, Z_{k-1}|s_{0:k}) = p(Z_{k-1}|s_{0:k})p(z_k|s_{0:k}) = p(z_k|s_k)p(Z_{k-1}|s_{0:k-1})$, $p(s_{0:k}) = p(s_k|s_{0:k-1})p(s_{0:k-1}) = p(s_k|s_{k-1})p(s_{0:k-1})$.

In practice, choosing the proposal distribution is important for a successful particle filtering approach. Usually, we can take $q(s_k|S_{k-1}, Z_k) = p(s_k|s_{k-1})$. Hence, sequential importance sampling is as follows:

$$w_k = w_{k-1}p(z_k|s_k). \tag{4.21}$$

This equation means that we can obtain the estimates of the importance weights in a recursive way under the constraint of Markov dynamic models. Moreover, the weight update is proportional to the likelihood when the proposal distribution is the prior system equation. Finally, we would like to point out that there are two fundamental assumptions of particle filtering: a first-order Markov process of states and observation models.

We summarize the **Basic Particle Filtering Algorithm** as follows:

1. **Initialization:** For $k = 0$, sample $N$ particles $s_0^i$ $(i = 0, \ldots, N-1)$ from $p(s_0)$;
2. **Important Sampling:** Sample $\tilde{s}_k^i$ from $p(s_k|s_{k-1}^i)$, then evaluate the importance weights $w_k^i = p(z_k|\tilde{s}_k^i)$, and normalize the importance weights $\widetilde{w}_k^j = w_k^j / \sum_{j=1}^N w_k^j$;
3. **Re-sampling:** According to the normalized importance weights $\widetilde{w}_k^i$, re-sample with replacement $N$ particles $s_{0:k}^i$ $(i = 0, \ldots, N-1)$ from the set $\tilde{s}_{0:k}^i$ $(i = 0, \ldots, N-1)$;
4. Then proceed to the Importance Sampling step, when the next measurement arrives.

### 4.4.2 Lane Model

In this approach, the lane tracking is formulated for the estimation of lane's parameters and vehicle's states. In this section, we introduce the lane model and the dynamic system model.

We represent the lane shape by a Taylor series expression of a clothoid [38, 43]

$$y(x) = y_0 + \tan(\phi) + \frac{a_0}{2}x^2 + \frac{a_1}{6}x^3, \tag{4.22}$$

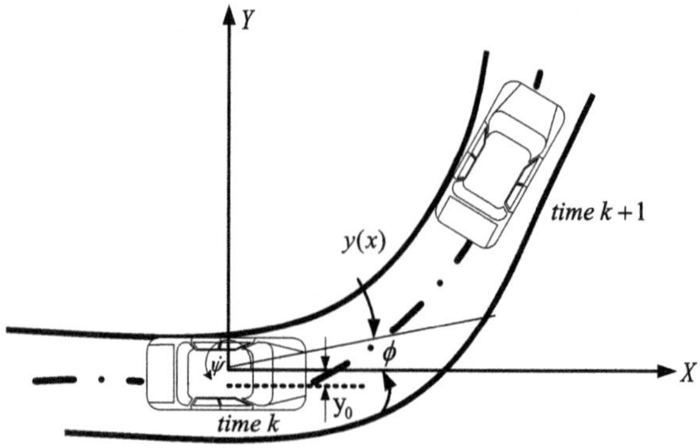


**Fig. 4.5** An illustration of a vehicle dynamic system model at different times

where $y$ is the lateral position of the road center relative to the vehicle, $x$ is the longitudinal distance ahead, $\phi$ is the pitch of the camera relative to the road surface, $a_0$ and $a_1$ are the curvature and curvature rate of the lanes.

### 4.4.3 Dynamic System Model

The lane tracking algorithm is based on a 4D state vector $s_k$

$$s_k = \left[y_0(k), \phi(k), a_0(k), a_1(k)\right]^T. \tag{4.23}$$

Now we have the dynamic system model:

$$\begin{bmatrix} y_0(k+1) \\ \phi(k+1) \\ a_0(k+1) \\ a_1(k+1) \end{bmatrix} = \begin{bmatrix} 1 & \Delta x & \frac{\Delta x^2}{2} & \frac{\Delta x^3}{6} \\ 0 & 1 & \Delta x & \frac{\Delta x^2}{2} \\ 0 & 0 & 1 & \Delta x \\ 0 & 0 & 0 & 1 \end{bmatrix} \begin{bmatrix} y_0(k) \\ \phi(k) \\ a_0(k) \\ a_1(k) \end{bmatrix} + \begin{bmatrix} 0 \\ -\Delta\psi_k \\ 0 \\ 0 \end{bmatrix}, \tag{4.24}$$

where $\Delta\psi_k$ is the yaw rate at time $k$. The vehicle dynamic system model is shown in Fig. 4.5.

### 4.4.4 The Imaging Model

Now, we have to build the dynamic system model. However, only the mapping model between image coordinates and world coordinates can affect state changes as an observation. The relationships between image coordinates $(u, v)$ and vehicle coordinates $(x, y)$ are [43]

$$\begin{cases} u = \frac{Y_c}{X_c} f_u = \frac{Y}{X\cos\phi + H\sin\phi} f_u \approx \frac{-y}{x\cos\phi + H\sin\phi}, \\ v = \frac{Z_c}{X_c} f_v = \frac{H\cos\phi - X\sin\phi}{X\cos\phi + H\sin\phi} f_v \approx \frac{H\cos\phi - x\sin\phi}{x\cos\phi + H\sin\phi}. \end{cases} \tag{4.25}$$

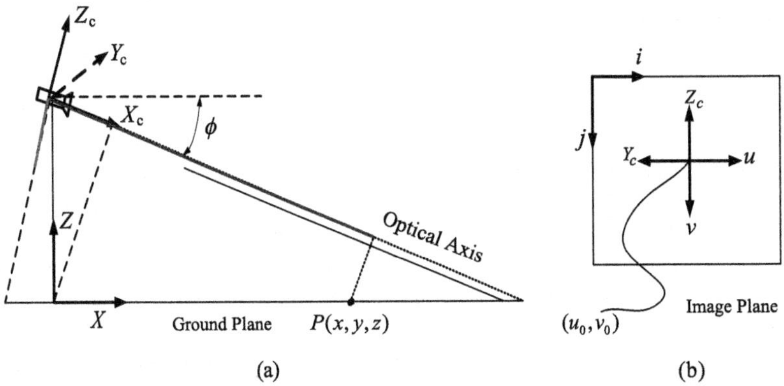


**Fig. 4.6** Vehicle, road and image coordinate systems. The road $y$-axis points into the page: (**a**) Geometric mapping between camera coordinates and world coordinates; (**b**) Image coordinates systems

Note that $Z_c$ denotes the red line in Fig. 4.6 and $X_c$ denotes the blue line. Moreover, the relationships between image coordinates and pixel coordinates are

$$u = \frac{i - u_0}{f_u}, \qquad v = \frac{j - v_0}{f_v}, \tag{4.26}$$

where $(u_0, v_0)$ is the principal point of the camera, and $f_u$ and $f_v$ are the effective focal lengths of the camera in the $i$ and $j$ directions, respectively. The relationship among vehicle coordinates, camera coordinates, and image coordinates is illustrated in Fig. 4.6.

The camera pitch $\phi$ used in (4.25) is calculated by

$$v_h = \frac{H\cos\phi - x\sin\phi}{x\cos\phi + H\sin\phi} = \frac{H/x - \tan\phi}{1 + H/x\tan\phi}; \tag{4.27}$$

when $x \to \infty$, $v_h$ can be represented as follows:

$$v_h = -\tan\phi, \tag{4.28}$$

where the $v_h$ is the $v$ coordinate on the horizontal line.

Also, the camera height can be calculated by

$$H = \frac{w\cos\phi}{I'_r - I'_l}, \tag{4.29}$$

where $I'_r$ and $I'_l$ are image gradient of the right and left lanes, respectively, $w$ is the lane width.

In this section, we need to calibrate camera intrinsic and external parameters: the principal point $(u_0, v_0)$, focal length $(f_u, f_v)$, and the pitch angle $\phi$ as described before. We use Caltech's camera calibration toolbox for Matlab to obtain those parameters [48].[3]

### 4.4.5 The Algorithm Implementation

The CONDENSATION algorithm [27] is used to estimate the shape of the road ahead of the vehicle. The basic idea is that the distribution is approximated by a set of $N$ 'particles', pairs $[s,\omega]$, $s$ is a state vector, and $\omega$ is a weight that reflects the plausibility of $s$ as a representation of the true state of the system. In this section, we will introduce several basic issues about the lane tracking implementation based on particle filtering.

#### 4.4.5.1 Factored Sampling

Let us first introduce the factorized sampling algorithm in order to represent successive image observations. For non-Gaussian observations from image sequences, as we have mentioned before, lane tracking is formulated as a problem of estimating the parameters $s(k)$. In this case, the posterior density represents all the knowledge about $s$ from the observed data. From the Bayes' rule, we obtain

$$p(s|z) = \eta p(z|s)p(s), \tag{4.30}$$

where $\eta$ is a normalization factor; we are usually not able to calculate it simply in a closed form. Hence, iterative sampling techniques can be used.

The factored sampling algorithm generates a random variate $s$ from a proposal distribution. First, we generate particles $\{s_k^{(0)},\dots,s_k^{(N-1)}\}$ from its prior probability $p(s)$ and its weight $\omega_k^n$ according to the likelihood $p(z|s_k^n)$ at time $k$ as follows:

$$\omega_k^n = \frac{p(z_k|s_k^{(n)})}{\sum_{j=0}^{N-1} p(z_k|s_k^{(j)})}. \tag{4.31}$$

Now, a re-sampling step is used to generate a new particle set $\{s_{k+1}^{\prime n}, i = 0,\dots,N-1\}$ as follows:

1. Generate a uniformly distributed random number $r \in [0,1]$;
2. Seek the smallest $j$ for which $c_k^j \geq r$;
3. Set $s_{k+1}^{\prime n} = s_k^{\prime j}$, where $c_k^n$ is the accumulated weight of particle $j$ at time $k$.

We would like to point out that the higher weight a particle has, the more likely it will be sampled. The weight $\omega_n^k$ effects the occurrence probability of the corresponding particle $s_k^n$ from the observation. When $N$ is sufficiently large, the samples

[3] http://www.vision.caltech.edu/bouguetj/calib_doc/.

**Fig. 4.7** The filtering result of a road image

will approach the posterior density $p(s_k^n|z_k)$. That is, when $N$ is large enough, the weighed average of all the particles will approach the precise state.

#### 4.4.5.2 The Observation and Measure Models

In lane tracking, we need to update the weights as in (4.31) using successive image observations. This procedure divides into two steps, generating observations and measuring the similarity between the extracted pixels and those from particles.

In the observation step, we directly extract lane pixel positions as image observations. Similar to [43], we extract lane markings from the red channel of our color images. Afterwards, a $3 \times 9$ filter kernel is used to extract lane marks

$$\begin{bmatrix} 1 & 3 & 5 & 7 & 9 & 7 & 5 & 3 & 1 \\ 1 & 3 & 5 & 7 & 9 & 7 & 5 & 3 & 1 \\ 1 & 3 & 5 & 7 & 9 & 7 & 5 & 3 & 1 \end{bmatrix}. \tag{4.32}$$

From Fig. 4.7, we can see that the lane marks are obviously better seen.

Let us denote the pixel from lanes object pixels. Furthermore, we search the nearest neighbors of the predicted pixels within object pixels, thus yielding the distance between the predicted pixels and the resulting object pixels, shown in Fig. 4.8. In practice, for each predicted pixel set from the corresponding particle, we search its object pixels in yellow and gray search windows, respectively. Finally, we obtain the distance from each predicted pixel to its object pixel.

After yielding the distance measures between the predicted pixels of each particle and the corresponding object pixels, we calculate the weights of each particle. Let $p_i(s_k^n)$ denote the $i$th predicted pixel from particle $s_k^n$ and let $\hat{p}_i(s_k^n)$ denote the corresponding object pixel. First, we sum the distances of particle $s_k^n$

$$\pi_n = \sum_i d\big(p_i\big(s_k^n, \hat{p}_i\big(s_k^n\big)\big)\big). \tag{4.33}$$

Then, we calculate the weight $\omega_{k+1}^n$ of each particle using its sum of distances

$$\omega_{k+1}^n = 1/\pi_n^2. \tag{4.34}$$

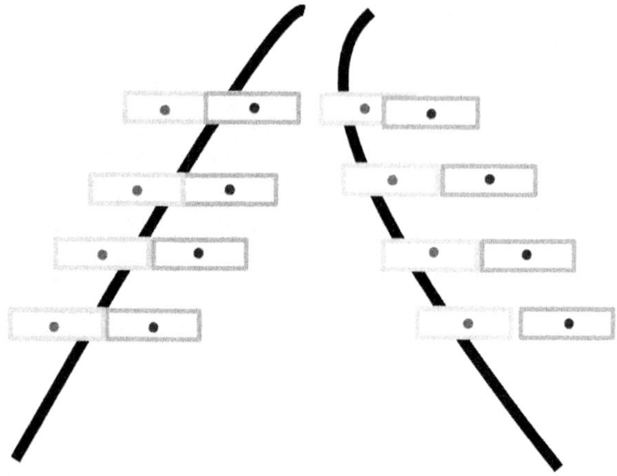

**Fig. 4.8** The search of object pixels: the *blue* and *red* pixels represent those from different particles

Finally, we normalize the weight so that $\sum_n \omega_{k+1}^{(n)} = 1$. Moreover, the cumulative weights $c_{k+1}^n$ are

$$c_{k+1}^n = c_{k+1}^{n-1} + \omega_{k+1}^n, \qquad c_{k+1}^0 = 0. \tag{4.35}$$

Here, a new particle set $\{s_{k+1}^n, \omega_{k+1}^n, c_{k+1}^n\}$ is generated.

According to the distances between each predicted pixel and its nearest neighbor within object pixels of each particle, the predicted pixels of each particle have different scores. Accumulating their scores generates the weight of each particle. Figure 4.9 (left) shows the weights of the predicted pixels.

Once having the $N$ particles, we calculate the state at time $k+1$ by the weighed average of all the particles

$$E[s_{k+1}] = \sum_{n=0}^{N-1} \omega_{k+1}^{(n)} s_{k+1}^{(n)}. \tag{4.36}$$

Figure 4.9 (right) shows the estimated results.

#### 4.4.5.3 The Algorithm Flow

We summarize the lane tracking algorithm based on particle filter as follows:

**Input:** A particle set $\{s_k^n, \omega_k^n, c_k^n\}_{n=0,\dots,N-1}$ at time $k$, and the observed image at time $k+1$;

**Iteration:** $(n = 0, \dots, N-1)$

**1. Sample Selection:** Select a sample $s_{k+1}^{\prime n}$ from the particle set based on particle weights $\{\omega_k^n\}$.

**2. Prediction by the Dynamic Evolution Model:** Equation (4.24) is used to predict a new particle $s_{k+1}^n$ from $s_{k+1}^{\prime n}$.

**3. Updating the Weights of Particles:** We evaluate the plausibility of the evolved particle by comparing the predicted pixels from the particle to object pixels

**Fig. 4.9** The predicted pixel distribution and their weights. *Darker color* indicates higher score. The *green lines* are estimated lane marks calculated from the weighed average of $N$ particles. So the *predicted points* which are closer to lane marks have higher scores

**Fig. 4.10** Lane tracking using the particle filtering approach

from a current observed image. Equation (4.34) can update the weight $\omega_{k+1}^n$ and the accumulative weight $c_{k+1}^n$ of the current particle.
**Calculating lane position at time $k+1$:** The lane position at time $k+1$ is calculated by (4.31).

Figure 4.10 shows the lane tracking results using the particle filtering approach.

## 4.5 Road Recognition Using a Mean Shift algorithm

In the previous section, we assumed that there exist multiple lane marks on the so-called structured roads, such as highways. Hence, we could define parameterized lane models and then estimate the parameters of lane marks. However, there are no visible lane marks on the unstructured roads, such as county roads [5]. In this case, we have to use other visual cues, such as textures, colors. For example, Rapidly Adapting Lateral Position Handler (RALPH) system [40] combines the color and the texture of a road to better recognize it. In this section, we use Mean Shift (MS)

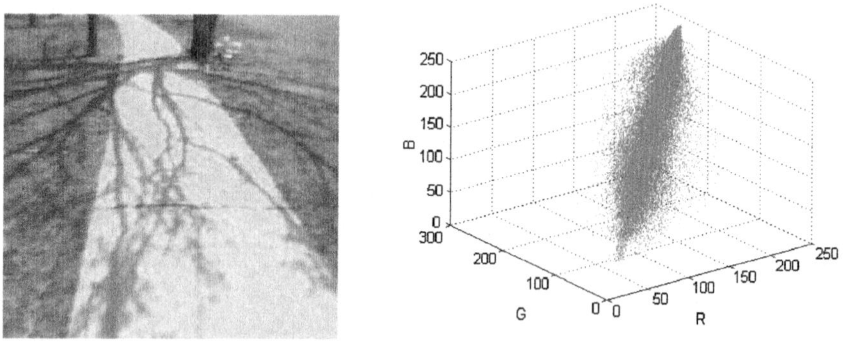


(a) The original road image with resolution of 256 × 256.

(b) The feature space distribution of (a).

**Fig. 4.11** The road image and its feature space distribution

algorithms to cluster road pixels and non-road pixels based on color and texture features, thus resulting in road recognition.

Feature space analysis approaches are widely used in low-level visual processing tasks [12], where probability density estimation is the most basic algorithm. The goal of feature space analysis is to seek significant features, space structures, and even subspaces. The denser regions in the feature space could correspond to important features, which leads to data clustering. The feature space analysis based on probability density estimation consists of two steps. The first step is to represent the feature spaces in some distributions. The most commonly-used feature space representation is the Gaussian Mixture Model (GMM) [7, 42]. However, the number of components is a prior in GMM. Hence, for arbitrarily structured feature spaces (shown in Fig. 4.11), we have to turn to nonparametric approaches which do not make assumptions. The second step is to seek significant features based the previous parametric/nonparametric approaches.

### *4.5.1 The Basic Mean Shift Algorithm*

Nowadays, mean shift algorithms are widely used in computer vision community as a robust feature space analysis approach, for example, in data clustering [10], image and video segmentation [12, 44], visual tracking [11, 14]. Originally, the mean shift algorithm was proposed as a nonparametric data clustering approach based on the gradient estimation of probability density functions (pdfs) by Fukunaga et al. in 1975 [20]. Later, Cheng further generalized and analyzed this algorithm and its properties [10], which now attracts more researchers working on its applications again. In computer vision community, Peter Meer and others first applied this algorithm to various computer vision tasks, image segmentation [12, 13], non-rigid object tracking [14]. The basic idea is to repeatedly move the nearby data points to their mode. Finally, the iteration procedure will converge to its global optimal solution [10]. In principal, the mean shift algorithm is an iterative multi-start global optimization approach [10, 18].

Given $N$ features $x_i \in \mathbb{R}^D$, $i = 0, 1, \ldots, N-1$, within a feature space, we estimate the pdf using a symmetric kernel density estimator:

$$\hat{p}_k(x) = \alpha \sum_{i=0}^{N-1} K(x, x_i, H) = \alpha \sum_{i=0}^{N-1} K\left(\|x - x_i\|^2, H\right), \tag{4.37}$$

where $\alpha = 1/(N\sqrt{H})$, $\int K(x)\,dx = 1$. In practice, we simplify the complexity of $H$ by taking $H = h^2\mathbf{I}$ and thus $\alpha = \frac{1}{Nh^D}$.

The gradient of (4.37) is

$$\nabla \hat{p}_K(x) = \alpha_1 \sum_{i=0}^{N-1} (x - x_i) K'\left(\|x - x_i\|^2, H\right), \tag{4.38}$$

where $\alpha_1$ is a normalization factor.

Now, defining a function $G(\|x - x_i\|^2, H) = -K'(\|x - x_i\|^2, H)$, we get

$$\nabla \hat{p}_K(x) = \alpha_2 \left( \sum_{i=0}^{N-1} G\left(\|x - x_i\|^2, H\right) \right) \left( \frac{\sum_{i=0}^{N-1} x_i G(\|x - x_i\|^2, H)}{\sum_{i=0}^{N-1} G(\|x - x_i\|^2, H)} - x \right), \tag{4.39}$$

where $G(\cdot) \geq 0$. In the above equation, the first item is $\hat{p}_G(x) = \sum_{i=0}^{N-1} G(\|x - x_i\|^2, H)$. Let us define

$$y_i = \frac{\sum_{i=0}^{N-1} x_i G(\|x - x_i\|^2, H)}{\sum_{i=0}^{N-1} G(\|x - x_i\|^2, H)}, \tag{4.40}$$

and thus the second item is $m_G(x) = y_i - x$. Actually, $y_i$ is the filtered result of $x_i$ by weighted neighbors within the feature space in mean shift filtering.

Therefore, we obtain the mean shift vector by

$$m_G(x) = \alpha_3 \frac{\nabla \hat{p}_K(x)}{\hat{p}_G(x)}, \tag{4.41}$$

where $\alpha_3$ is a normalization factor. From (4.41), we can see that (i) the mean shift vector is proportional to the normalized density gradient w.r.t. $k$, (ii) the normalized weighted mean $y_i$ w.r.t. the kernel $G$ is a weighted average within the neighbors of $x_i$, (iii) the mean shift vector moves always to the maximum gradient direction of the density.

Now we discuss kernel functions in mean shift algorithms. The $D$-dimensional multivariate Gaussian kernel is

$$K_N(x) = \frac{1}{\sqrt{2\pi D}} \exp\left(-\frac{1}{2}\|x\|^2\right). \tag{4.42}$$

Another popular kernel is the Epanechnikov Kernel [12]

$$K_E = \begin{cases} \frac{d+2}{2C_d} \times (1 - \|x\|^2) & \text{if } \|x\| < 1, \\ 0 & \text{otherwise.} \end{cases} \tag{4.43}$$

Note that in the mean shift algorithm, the above two are radially symmetric kernels. Furthermore, we will use a two-dimensional kernel. Assuming an image is a two-dimensional lattice of $D$-dimensional pixels, the multi-variate kernel is represented as [12, 13]:

$$K(x, h_s, h_r) = \frac{C}{h_s^2 h_r^D} K\left(\left\|\frac{x^s}{h_s}\right\|^2\right) K\left(\left\|\frac{x^r}{h_r}\right\|^2\right), \tag{4.44}$$

where $h = (h_s, h_r)$ is the kernel bandwidth, $C$ is a constant, $x^s$ and $x^r$ are the position part and the range part of a feature vector.

In the following section, we will introduce different computer vision tasks using basic mean shift algorithms.

### 4.5.2 *Various Applications of the Mean Shift Algorithm*

**Mean Shift Clustering** The most basic application of mean shift algorithms is data clustering. Given feature vectors $x_i$ and their resulting labels $z_i$, we can use the following procedure to filter feature vectors:

- Initialization: $y_{i,1} = x_i$;
- Repeat calculating $y_{i,k+1}$ from $y_{i,k}$ using kernel $G$ at time $k+1$ as follows:

$$y_{i,k+1} = \frac{\sum_{i=0}^{N-1} y_{i,k} G(\|x - y_{i,k}\|^2, H)}{\sum_{i=0}^{N-1} G(\|x - y_{i,k}\|^2, H)}. \tag{4.45}$$

  Finally, we get $y_{i,\infty}$, thus yielding cluster centers $y_l$, $l = 0, 1, \dots, L-1$ until coverage.
- Label features: $z_i = \{x_i, y_{i,\infty}, y_l\}$.

**The Mean Shift Segmentation** Similar to mean shift clustering, we assume that $x_i$ and $y_i$ are the feature vectors and the filtered vectors. The goal of image segmentation is to yield the labels $l$, $l = 0, 1, \dots, L-1$ of all pixels. The detailed algorithm flow is as follows:

- Extract feature vectors $x_i$, $i = 0, 1, \dots, N-1$ of all pixels.
- Implement mean shift filtering over all pixels $x_i$, and thus generate the clusters

$$\{y_l\}, \quad l = 0, 1, \dots, L-1. \tag{4.46}$$

- Assign labels $l = \{c | y_{i,\infty} \in y_c\}$.
- Post-processing: remove image regions with less than the predefined number of pixels.

**Mean Shift Tracking** In principal, given the target position in the previous frame, visual tracking is to estimate the target position in the current frame. Let $\hat{q}_x$ represent the density function of the target model based on feature $x_i$, and let $\hat{p}_x(y)$ be the pdf of a candidate target at position $y$. Hence, mean shift visual tracking is to seek the position $y$ which is the most similar to $\hat{q}_x$ by [14]

$$\hat{y} = \underset{y}{\operatorname{argmin}} \sqrt{1 - \rho\big(\hat{p}_x(y), \hat{q}_x\big)}. \tag{4.47}$$

The basic algorithm flow of mean shift tracking is as follows:

- Detect the initial position $\hat{y}_0$ of the target in the first frame and thus compute the target distribution $\{\hat{q}_u\}$, $u = 0, 1, \dots, m-1$.
- Initialize the target position at frame $k$ with $\hat{y}_0$ and then calculate the distribution $\{\hat{p}_u(\hat{y}_0)\}$, $u = 0, 1, \dots, m-1$, where the total distribution refers to [14]. Hence, we evaluate

$$\rho\big[\hat{p}(\hat{y}_0), \hat{y}\big] = \sum_{u=0}^{m-1} \sqrt{\hat{p}_u(\hat{y}_0)\hat{q}_u}. \tag{4.48}$$

- Calculate the weight of each position $x_i$, $i = 0, 1, \dots, n_n - 1$ of candidate targets

$$w_i = \sum \delta\big[b(x_i) - u\big] \sqrt{\frac{\hat{q}_u}{\hat{p}_u(\hat{y}_0)}}, \tag{4.49}$$

where $u$ is color value, $\delta(\cdot)$ is the Kronecker delta function, $b(x_i)$ is the histogram bin corresponding to the color value of pixel $x_i$.
- Calculate the new position

$$\hat{y}_1 = \frac{\sum_{i=0}^{n_h-1} x_i w_i G(\|\hat{y}_0 - x_i\|^2, H)}{\sum_{i=0}^{n_h-1} w_i G(\|\hat{y}_0 - x_i\|^2, H)}, \tag{4.50}$$

and $\{\hat{p}_u(\hat{y}_1)\}$, $u = 0, 1, \dots, m-1$, and also $\rho[\hat{p}(\hat{y}_1), \hat{q}] = \sum_{u=0}^{m-1} \sqrt{\hat{p}_u(\hat{y}_1)\hat{q}_u}$.
- While $\rho[\hat{p}(\hat{y}_1), \hat{q}] < \rho[\hat{p}(\hat{y}_0), \hat{q}]$
  Do $\hat{y}_1 \leftarrow \frac{1}{2}(\hat{y}_0 + \hat{y}_1)$
- If $\|\hat{y}_1 - \hat{y}_0\| < \varepsilon$, stop; Otherwise, $\hat{y}_0 = \hat{y}_1$, and go to Step 2.

### *4.5.3 The Road Recognition Algorithm*

The commonly-used color spaces are *RGB*, *HSV*, *CIE* − *XYZ*, and *CIE* − $L^*u^*v^*$, which are all applications dependant. The *RGB* color space is a linear color space which is commonly used for display. Similar to [12], we use $L^*u^*v^*$ to represent pixel features, since this color space is good for perceiving uniform color spaces.

The $L^*u^*v^*$ color space is transformed from the $RGB$ color space by

$$\begin{cases} L^* = 116 \times \sqrt[3]{\frac{Y}{Y_n}} - 16, \\ u^* = 13L^*(u' - u_0), \\ v^* = 13L^*(v' - v_0), \end{cases} \tag{4.51}$$

where $Y/Y_0 > 0$, $u' = \frac{4Z}{Z+15Y+3Z}$, $v' = \frac{6Y}{Z+15Y+3Z}$, and

$$\begin{bmatrix} Z \\ Y \\ X \end{bmatrix} = \begin{bmatrix} 0.607 & 0.174 & 0.2 \\ 0.229 & 0.587 & 0.114 \\ 0 & 0.066 & 1.116 \end{bmatrix} \begin{bmatrix} R \\ G \\ B \end{bmatrix}. \tag{4.52}$$

Regarding this space, we can use the following equation to measure color distance:

$$\triangle E = \sqrt{(\triangle L^*)^2 + (\triangle u^*)^2 + (\triangle v^*)^2}. \tag{4.53}$$

We summarize the road recognition using mean shift segmentation as follows:

- Down-sampled original images for reducing computational complexity.
- Extract pixel features using $L^*u^*v^*$ color spaces.
- Segment image using mean shift segment algorithms.
- Remove the regions which contain fewer than the predefined number of pixels.
- Recognize road regions using a road reference region; here we use a small image region before a vehicle as a road region.

### 4.5.4 Experimental Results and Analysis

We evaluate the road recognition algorithm on CMU's road dataset,[4] which are series of road images taken from various Navlabs [23].

Figure 4.12 shows a road image captured on a sunny day. Figure 4.12(a) is an original image with resolution 256 × 240, Figs. 4.12(b) and 4.12(c) correspond to the results of using mean shift segmentation when *region_max* = 10 and 100, respectively. Figure 4.13 shows feature space distributions after using median filtering and mean shift filtering. Similar to Fig. 4.12, Fig. 4.14 presents the results of using mean shift segmentation but on a cloudy image.

From the experiments above, we can see that: (i) the feature space analysis using mean shift algorithm is robust to different illumination; (ii) the performance of mean shift filtering is remarkably better than that of median filtering; (iii) post-processing can improve the recognition results.

[4]http://vasc.ri.cmu.edu/idb/html/road/index.html.

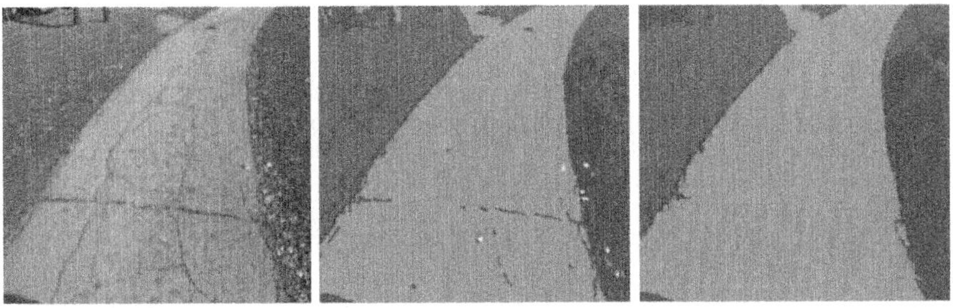

(a) The original image 256 × 240.

(b) When *Region_Max* = 10 the identified traffic available areas.

(c) When *Region_Max* = 100 the identified traffic available areas.

**Fig. 4.12** Sunny country road images

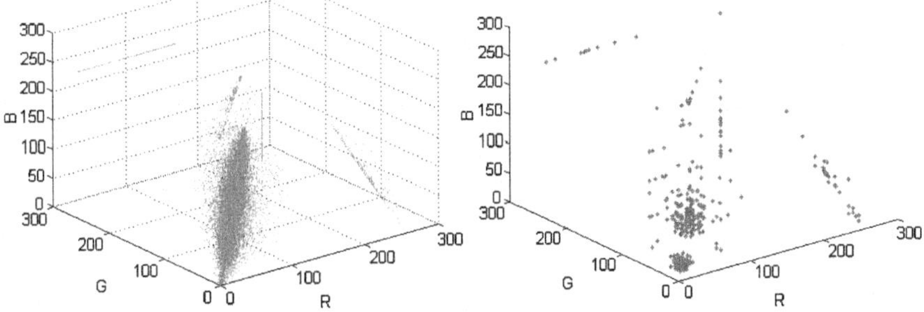


(a) The mode distribution after of the median filter.

(b) The mode distribution after mean shift.

**Fig. 4.13** The feature space distributions after using median filtering and mean shift filtering

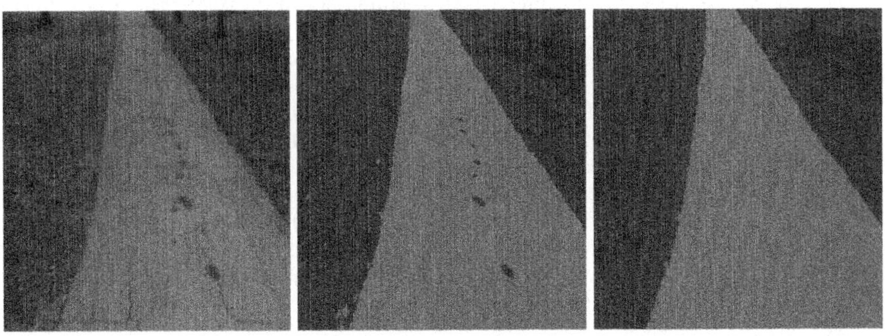

(a) The original image with resolution of 256 × 240.

(b) *Region_Max* = 10; the identified available areas for traffic.

(c) *Region_Max* = 100; the identified available areas for traffic.

**Fig. 4.14** The lane detection on cloudy country road images

## References


1. Apostoloff, N., Zelinsky, A.: Robust vision based lane tracking using multiple cues and particle filtering. In: Proc. of the IEEE Intelligent Vehicles Symposium (2003)
2. Arulampalam, M.S., Maskell, S., Gordon, N., Clapp, T.: A tutorial on particle filters for online nonlinear/non-Gaussian Bayesian tracking. IEEE Trans. Signal Process., **50**(2), 174–188 (2002)
3. Ballard, D.H.: Generalizing the Hough transform to detect arbitrary shapes. Pattern Recognit., **13**(2), 111–122 (1981)
4. Bertozzi, M., Broggi, A.: GOLD: a parallel real-time stereo vision system for generic obstacle and lane detection. IEEE Trans. Image Process., **7**(1), 62–81 (1998)
5. Bertozzi, M., Broggi, A.: GOLD: a parallel real-time stereo vision system for generic obstacle and lane detection. IEEE Trans. Image Process., **7**(1), 62–81 (2002)
6. Beucher, S., Bilodeau, M.: Road segmentation and obstacle detection by a fast watershed transformation. In: Proc. of the IEEE Intelligent Vehicles Symposium (1994)
7. Bishop, C.M.: Pattern Recognition and Machine Learning, vol. 4. Springer, New York (2006)
8. Broggi, A.: Automatic Vehicle Guidance: The Experience of the ARGO Autonomous Vehicle. World Scientific, Singapore (1999)
9. Cheng, H., Zheng, N., Zhang, X., Qin, J., Van de Wetering, H.: Interactive road situation analysis for driver assistance and safety warning systems: framework and algorithms. IEEE Trans. Intell. Transp. Syst., **8**(1), 157–167 (2007)
10. Cheng, Y.: Mean shift, mode seeking, and clustering. IEEE Trans. Pattern Anal. Mach. Intell., **17**(8), 790–799 (1995)
11. Collins, R.T.: Mean-shift blob tracking through scale space. In: Proc. of the IEEE Computer Society Conference on Computer Vision and Pattern Recognition (2003)
12. Comaniciu, D., Meer, P.: Mean shift analysis and applications. In: Proc. of the IEEE International Conference on Computer Vision (2002)
13. Comaniciu, D., Ramesh, V., Meer, P.: The variable bandwidth mean shift and data-driven scale selection. In: Proc. of the IEEE International Conference on Computer Vision (2002)
14. Comaniciu, D., Ramesh, V., Meer, P.: Kernel-based object tracking. IEEE Trans. Pattern Anal. Mach. Intell., **25**(5), 564–575 (2003)
15. Doucet, A., De Freitas, N., Gordon, N.: Sequential Monte Carlo Methods in Practice. Springer, Berlin (2001)
16. Ecabert, O., Thiran, J.P.: Adaptive Hough transform for the detection of natural shapes under weak affine transformations. Pattern Recognit. Lett., **25**(12), 1411–1419 (2004)
17. Fardi, B., Wanielik, G.: Hough transformation based approach for road border detection in infrared images. In: IEEE Intelligent Vehicles Symposium (2004)
18. Fashing, M., Tomasi, C.: Mean shift is a bound optimization. IEEE Trans. Pattern Anal. Mach. Intell., **27**(3), 471–474 (2005)
19. Forsyth, D.A., Ponce, J.: Computer Vision: A Modern Approach (2002). Prentice Hall Professional Technical Reference
20. Fukunaga, K., Hostetler, L.D.: The estimation of the gradient of a density function, with applications in pattern recognition. IEEE Trans. Inf. Theory, **21**(1), 32–40 (1975)
21. Gern, A., Moebus, R., Franke, U.: Vision-based lane recognition under adverse weather conditions using optical flow. In: IEEE Intelligent Vehicle Symposium (2002)
22. Hashimoto, K., Nakayama, S., Saito, T., Ishida, S., Unuora, K., Ishii, J., Oono, N., Okada, Y.: An image processing architecture and a motion control method for an autonomous vehicle. In: Proc. of the Intelligent Vehicles Symposium. IEEE, New York (2002)
23. Heikkila, J., Silven, O.: A four-step camera calibration procedure with implicit image correction. In: IEEE Conference on Computer Vision and Pattern Recognition (1997)
24. Herman, M., Raviv, D., Schneiderman, H., Nashman, M.: Visual road following without 3D reconstruction. In: Proceedings of SPIE (1994)
25. Ieng, S.S., Tarel, J.P., Labayrade, R.: On the design of a single lane-markings detectors regardless the on-board camera's position. In: Proc. of the IEEE Intelligent Vehicles Symposium (2003)

26. Inglebert, C.: Road line tracking: an approach based on spatio-temporal surface. In: Proc. of the IAPR International Conference on Pattern Recognition. IEEE, New York (2002)
27. Isard, M., Blake, A.: Condensation—conditional density propagation for visual tracking. Int. J. Comput. Vis., **29**(1), 5–28 (1998)
28. Kluge, K.: Extracting road curvature and orientation from image edge points without perceptual grouping into features. In: Proc. of the Intelligent Vehicles Symposium. IEEE, New York (2002)
29. Li, Q., Zheng, N., Cheng, H.: An adaptive approach to lane markings detection. In: Proc. of the IEEE Intelligent Transportation Systems (2005)
30. Liu, T., Zheng, N., Cheng, H., Xing, Z.: A novel approach of road recognition based on deformable template and genetic algorithm. In: Proc. of the IEEE International Conference on Intelligent Transportation Systems, pp. 1251–1256 (2003)
31. Luong, Q.T., Weber, J., Koller, D., Malik, J.: An integrated stereo-based approach to automatic vehicle guidance. In: Proc. of the IEEE International Conference on Computer Vision (2002)
32. McCall, J.C., Trivedi, M.M.: An integrated, robust approach to lane marking detection and lane tracking. In: IEEE Intelligent Vehicles Symposium (2004)
33. McCall, J.C., Trivedi, M.M.: Video-based lane estimation and tracking for driver assistance: survey, system, and evaluation. IEEE Trans. Intell. Transp. Syst., **7**(1), 20–37 (2006)
34. McDonald, J.: Detecting and tracking road markings using the Hough transform. In: Proc. of the Irish Machine Vision and Image Processing Conference (2001)
35. Nedevschi, S., Schmidt, R., Graf, T., Danescu, R., Frentiu, D., Marita, T., Oniga, F., Pocol, C.: 3D lane detection system based on stereovision. In: Proc. of the IEEE International Conference on Intelligent Transportation Systems (2004)
36. Nedevschi, S., Schmidt, R., Graf, T., Danescu, R., Frentiu, D., Marita, T., Oniga, F., Pocol, C.: 3D lane detection system based on stereovision. In: Proc. of the IEEE Conference on Intelligent Transportation Systems (2005)
37. Paetzold, F., Franke, U., Von Seelen, W.: Lane recognition in urban environment using optimal control theory. In: Proc. of the IEEE Intelligent Vehicles Symposium (2000)
38. Peterson, K., Ziglar, J., Rybski, P.E.: Fast feature detection and stochastic parameter estimation of road shape using multiple LIDAR. In: IEEE/RSJ International Conference on Intelligent Robots and Systems (2008)
39. Pomerleau, D.A.: Progress in neural network-based vision for autonomous robot driving. In: Proc. of the Intelligent Vehicles' 92 Symposium (1992)
40. Pomerleau, D.: RALPH: rapidly adapting lateral position handler. In: Proc. of the IEEE Intelligent Vehicles Symposium (1995)
41. Redmill, K.A., Upadhya, S., Krishnamurthy, A., Ozguner, U.: A lane tracking system for intelligent vehicle applications. In: Proc. of the IEEE International Conference on Intelligent Transportation Systems (2001)
42. Reynolds, D.A., Quatieri, T.F., Dunn, R.B.: Speaker verification using adapted Gaussian mixture models. Digit. Signal Process., **10**(1–3), 19–41 (2000)
43. Southall, B., Taylor, C.: Stochastic road shape estimation. In: Proc. of the IEEE International Conference on Computer Vision (2002)
44. Wang, J., Thiesson, B., Xu, Y., Cohen, M.: Image and video segmentation by anisotropic kernel mean shift. In: ECCV 2004, pp. 238–249 (2004)
45. Wang, Y., Teoh, E.K., Shen, D.: Lane detection and tracking using B-Snake. Image Vis. Comput., **22**(4), 269–280 (2004)
46. Youchun, X., Rongben, W., Shouwen, J.: A vision navigation algorithm based on linear lane model. In: Proc. of the IEEE Intelligent Vehicles Symposium (2002)
47. Yu, B., Jain, A.K.: Lane boundary detection using a multiresolution Hough transform. In: Proc. of the IEEE International Conference on Image Processing (2002)
48. Zhang, Z.: Flexible camera calibration by viewing a plane from unknown orientations. In: Proc. of the IEEE International Conference on Computer Vision (1999)
49. Zheng, N.N., Tang, S., Cheng, H., Li, Q., Lai, G., Wang, F.W.: Toward intelligent driver-assistance and safety warning system. IEEE Intell. Syst., **19**(2), 8–11 (2004)

# Chapter 5
# Vehicle Detection and Tracking

## 5.1 Introduction

Statistics shows that about 60% of the rear-end crash accidents can be avoided if the driver has additional warning time. According to the Ministry of Public Safety of P.R. China, there were 567,753 reported road traffic accidents in 2004, among those about 80% of the severe police-reported traffic accidents were vehicle–vehicle crashes. Almost two-fifths of these crashes resulted in an injury, with over 2% of the total crashes resulting in a death. Clearly, vehicle detection is an important research area of intelligent transportation systems [2, 11, 20]. It is being used in, among others, adaptive cruise control (ACC), driver assistance systems, automated visual traffic surveillance (AVTS), and self-guided vehicles. However, robust vehicle detection in real world traffic scenes is challenging.

Currently, IDASW systems based on radars have a higher cost than those based on machine vision, while having narrow field of view and bad lateral resolution. In Adaptive Cruise Control (ACC) systems, a camera can detect the cut-in and overtaking vehicle from the adjacent lane earlier than a radar. Due to these reasons, it is more difficult to apply such radar-based systems into practical IDASW systems. Consequently, robust and real time vehicle detection in video attracts more attention of scholars all over the world [2, 4, 14].

To detect on-road vehicle in time, this chapter introduces a multi-resolution hypothesis-validation structure. Inspired by A. Broggio [2], we extract three ROIs: a near one, one in the middle, and a far one, from a $640 \times 480$ image. His approach uses fixed regions at the cost of flexibility, we remove this limitation and build a simple and efficient hypothesis-validation structure which consists of the three steps described below:

1. ROI determination: We generate ROI candidates using a vanishing point of the road in the original image.
2. Vehicle hypothesis generation for each ROI using horizontal and vertical edge detection: We create a multi-resolution vehicle hypothesis based on the preceding candidate regions. From the analysis of edge histograms, we generate hypotheses for each ROI and combine them into a single list.

H. Cheng, *Autonomous Intelligent Vehicles*,
Advances in Computer Vision and Pattern Recognition,
DOI 10.1007/978-1-4471-2280-7_5, 

3. Hypothesis validation using Gabor features and SVM classifiers: We conduct vehicle validation using the boosted Gabor features of 9 sub-windows and the SVM classifiers. According to the judging of the classifiers, we determine whether hypotheses represent a vehicle or a non-vehicle.

## 5.2 Related Work

Hypotheses are generated using some simple features, such as color, horizontal and/or vertical edges, symmetry [2, 5], motion, and stereo visual cue. Zehang Sun proposed a multi-scale hypothesis method in which the original image was down-sampled to $320 \times 240$, $160 \times 120$, and $80 \times 60$. His vehicle hypotheses were generated by combining the horizontal and vertical edges of these three levels, and this multi-scale method greatly reduced random noise. This approach can generate multiple-hypothesis objects, but a near vehicle may prevent a far vehicle from being detected. As a result, the method fails to generate the corresponding hypothesis of the far vehicle, reducing the vehicle detection rate.

B. Leibe et al. seated a video-based 3D dynamic scene analysis system from a moving vehicle [9] which integrated scene geometry estimation, 2D vehicle and pedestrian detection, 3D localization and trajectory estimation. Impressively, this paper presented a multi-view/multi-category object detection approach in a real world traffic scene. Furthermore, 2D vehicle pedestrians detection is converted into 3D observation.

Vehicle symmetry is an important cue in vehicle detection and tracking. Inspired by the voting of Hough Transform, Yue Du et al. proposed a vehicle following approach by finding the symmetry axis of a vehicle [5]; however, their approach has several limitations, such as large computing burden, and it only generates one object hypothesis using the best symmetry. Alberto Broggi introduced a multi-resolution vehicle detection approach, and proposed dividing the image into three fixed ROIs: one near the host car, one far from the host car, and one in the middle [2]. This approach overcomes the limit of only being able to detect a single vehicle in the predefined region of the image, but it needs to compute the symmetry axis, making it not real-time.

D. Gabor first proposed the 1D Gabor function in 1946 and J.G. Daugman extended it to 2D later. In fact, a Gabor filter is a local bandpass filter that can reach the theoretical limit for the spatial domain and the frequency domain simultaneously. Consequently, Gabor filters have been successfully applied for object representation in various computer vision applications, such as texture segmentation and recognition [18], face recognition [19], scene recognition, and vehicle detection [14].

The basic issue of a Gabor filter is how to select the parameters of a filter that responds mainly to an interesting object, such as a vehicle or a pedestrian. Accurate detection only occurs if the parameters defining Gabor filters are well selected. Three main approaches have been proposed in the literature for selecting Gabor filters for object representation: manual selection, Gabor filter bank design (including filter design) [18], and a learning approach [13, 14, 16, 19]. In [1], Ilkka Autio proposed an approach for manual selection: An initial set of Gabor filters were experimentally selected from a larger set and then manually tuned. In general, a Gabor filter bank design defines a small filter pool, and determines the parameters of its filters independent of the application domain; moreover, the bandwidth of those Gabor filter design approaches cannot be determined autonomously. In image browsing and retrieval, a strategy is used to ensure that the half-peak magnitude support of the filter responses in the frequency domain touch each other by using a filter bank with 6 directions and 4 scales to compute the features of a texture [12]. Due to independence of the filter bank and the application domain, such an approach can be used for object classification, detection and tracking. The main problems of this filter design approach are small filter pool sizes, no prior knowledge, and poor performance. Learning-based Gabor filter design approaches select the Gabor filters according to its application domain. Du-Ming Tsai proposed an optimization algorithm for Gabor filters using a simulated annealing approach to obtain the best Gabor filter in texture segmentation [16]. A face recognition application using a strong classifier cascaded by weak classifiers was proposed by S.Z. Li; in his approach, weak classifiers were constructed based on both the magnitude and phase features from Gabor filters [19].

In terms of vehicle detection, Alberto Broggi introduced a multi-resolution vehicle detection approach, and proposed dividing the image into three fixed ROIs [2]. His approach allows detecting multiple vehicles in a predefined region. However, it uses a symmetry axis for detecting vehicles that is not only time-consuming to compute but symmetry features are somewhat problematic. In [14], Zehang Sun proposed an Evolutionary Gabor Filter Optimization (EGFO) approach for vehicle detection, and used the statistical features of the response of selected Gabor filters to classify the test image using a trained SVM classifier. Although good performance has been reported, EGFO has large computational cost for the selection of a Gabor filter. Moreover, each Gabor filter is optimized for a complete image, but it is applied to each sub-window of a test image, which reduces the quality of the representation.

The requirements of Vehicle Active Safety Systems (VASS) are strict with respect to the time performance for pedestrian detection and vehicle detection. Accordingly, in our approach we detect vehicles only in ROIs, allowing us to make a real-time implementation. The ROI approach largely prevents a near car from hiding a far car. All the hypotheses are generated in these regions. The positions of vehicles are validated by SVM classifiers and Gabor features.

## 5.3 Generating Candidate ROIs

Inspired by A. Broggio [2], we extract three ROIs: a near one, one in the middle, and a far one from a $640 \times 480$ image. But his approach uses fixed regions at the cost of flexibility. In our approach, ROIs are extracted using lane markings. In a structured lane, we detect the vanishing point using the lane edges. For the consideration of real-time processing, we use a simple vanishing point detector rather than a complex one. Discontinuity and noise related problems can be solved by combining, for

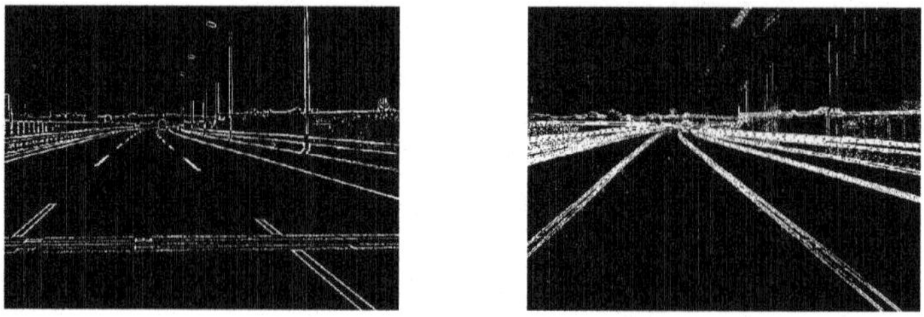

(a) Lane edge using single frame. (b) Overlapping of lane edge.

**Fig. 5.1** Edge detection results using single frame and multi-frame

instance, 10 subsequent images (see Fig. 5.1(a)). Edge detection is done on combined images consisting of 10 overlapping subsequent images, and the equations of two lanes are deduced from a voting procedures like HT by analyzing horizontal and vertical edges. Four random points $P_{di}$, $d = l$ or $r$; $i = 0, \ldots, 3$, are selected on each lane line, and each tangent direction of two points (shown in (5.1)) between the closest 3 points

$$\{P_{di}, P_{dj}\}; \quad d = r \text{ or } l; \quad i, j \in \{0, 1, 2, 3\}; \quad i < j; \quad |j - i| \leq 2, \tag{5.1}$$

is obtained by

$$\theta_{dij} = \overrightarrow{P_{di} P_{dj}}.$$

The tangent directions of two lane lines are calculated using the average value of the above tangent angles and are described by

$$\bar{\theta}_d = \frac{\theta_{d01} + \theta_{d02} + \theta_{d12} + \theta_{d13} + \theta_{d23}}{5}, \quad d = r \text{ or } l. \tag{5.2}$$

Combining the average coordinates of 4 interesting points $\bar{P}_d = \frac{1}{4} \sum_{i=0}^{3} P_{di}$ with the average tangent angles $\bar{\theta}_d$, we can get the equations of two lane lines. The intersection point of the two lines is an approximation of the vanishing point; see Fig. 5.2. Next we consider how to extract ROIs from the original image. For the consideration of vehicle height and the camera parameters, the top boundaries of all the ROIs are 10 pixels higher than the vertical coordinates of the vanishing point. From the analysis of the camera parameters and image resolution, the heights of the near, middle, and far ROIs are 160, 60, and 30 pixels, respectively. The left and right boundaries of the near ROI are those of the image. The distance between the left boundary of the middle ROI and that of the image is just one-third of the distance between the vanishing point and the left boundary of the image, and the right one of middle ROI is determined similarly. The distance between the left boundary of the far ROI and that of image is two-thirds of the distance between the vanishing point and the left boundary of image, as well as the distance between the right boundary of the far ROI and that of the image. Figure 5.2(b) shows the results of each ROI.

(a) Linking lines between interesting points.

(b) Division of ROI.

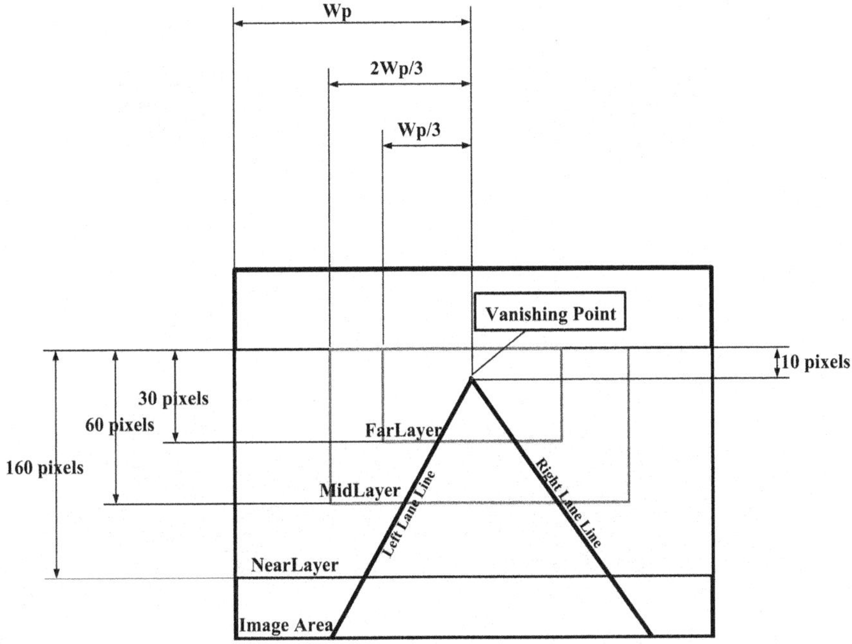


(c) Lane ROI generation.

**Fig. 5.2** Vanishing point and ROI generation

## 5.4 Multi-resolution Vehicle Hypothesis

For traditional approaches, the edges of small objects cover those of a large one; Fig. 5.3(b) is the result of a global histogram of horizontal and vertical edges and shows the edge histogram without a peak for the small vehicle. Based on the preceding candidate regions, the histogram of a ROI shows a peak for a small object, shown in Fig. 5.4. The analysis of the peaks and valleys of an edge histogram results in several rectangles, and each one represents a vehicle hypothesis. We use prior knowledge to eliminate some hypotheses. The minimum width of a vehicle can be set for each ROI. If the width of a hypothesis is smaller than this width, the

(a) Original image. (b) Edge histogram.

**Fig. 5.3** Global statistical histogram of horizontal and vertical edges

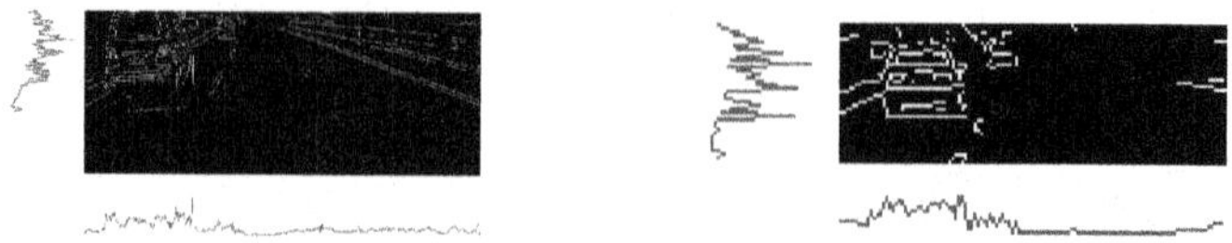

(a) Near layers image. (b) Far layer image.

**Fig. 5.4** Histogram of horizontal and vertical edges for the near and far ROIs

(a) Hypothesis generation result unusing ROI. (b) Hypothesis generation result using ROI.

**Fig. 5.5** Comparison of hypothesis generation results

hypothesis will be eliminated. Additionally, the aspect ratio (width/height) of vehicles is in a certain range; we assume this range to be [0.67, 2.2]. Rectangles with other ratios are eliminated. Since the histogram is made by extracting edges from the ROIs and other objects, like power cables and traffic signs above the road which are not in the ROIs, they do not disturb the edge histogram, reducing the false positive rate (see Fig. 5.5). The coordinates of all hypothesis objects will be translated into the coordinates of the original image, and then the hypotheses of different ROIs may be overlapping. According to the distance between two rectangles, $d(r_1, r_2)$, we can judge if the two rectangles ought to be incorporated into one. Equation (5.3) defines the distance between rectangles $r_1$ and $r_2$, and here $(x_{ij}, y_{ij})$ are the coordinates of the $j$th vertex of the $i$th rectangle, $i = 0, 1$; $j = 0, 1, 2, 3$. Through the above process, we finish the generation of vehicle hypotheses:

$$
\begin{aligned}
&d(r_0, r_1) = \|r_0 - r_1\|_2,\\
&r_i = (x_{i0}, y_{i0}, x_{i1}, y_{i1}, x_{i2}, y_{i2}, x_{i3}, y_{i3}), \quad i = 0, 1.
\end{aligned}
\tag{5.3}
$$

In conclusion, in our multi-resolution hypothesis generation approach, the ROIs complement each other; moreover, appropriate constraints improve the search efficiency, which greatly reduces the computing burden of hypothesis generation. Note that the heuristic multi-resolution works well in real-time though an Efficient Subwindows Search (ESS) which was proposed to localize objects using branch-and-bound optimizing algorithms [8].

## 5.5 Vehicle Validation using Gabor Features and SVM

After vehicle hypothesis generation, we are ready to validate the hypotheses. The preprocessing of the original image includes image scaling to 32 × 32, smoothing, histogram equalization, and image division. Afterwards, the vehicle can be represented with Gabor features, and the feature vector of a vehicle is input for the SVM classifier. According to the judging of the classifier, we determine that the hypothesis represents a vehicle or a non-vehicle.

### 5.5.1 Vehicle Representation

We first introduce some necessary definitions for Gabor filters and basic concepts for vehicle representation. The 2D Gabor function can be defined as follows:

$$
G_{\{f,\varphi,\sigma_u,\sigma_v\}}(u, v) = \frac{1}{2\pi\sigma_u\sigma_v} \exp\left[-\frac{1}{2}\left(\frac{U^2}{\sigma_u^2} + \frac{V^2}{\sigma_v^2}\right)\right] \exp[2\pi j f U], \tag{5.4}
$$

where

$$
\begin{cases}
U = (u, v)(\cos\varphi, \sin\varphi),\\
V = (-u, v)(\sin\varphi, \cos\varphi).
\end{cases}
$$

Here $f$ means the normalized spatial frequency of a complex sinusoidal signal modulating Gaussian function, $\varphi$ is the direction of a Gabor filter, $\sigma_u$ and $\sigma_v$ are the scale parameters of the filter. Therefore, $\{f, \varphi, \sigma_u, \sigma_v\}$ can represent the parameters of a Gabor filter. Actually, a Gabor filter is a bandpass filter, and the first step of vehicle detection is to select the Gabor filters strongly responding to the detected object.

Gabor features can be obtained by convolving the input image $I(u, v)((u, v) \in \Omega$, where $\Omega$ is the image pixel set) and a 2D Gabor filter $g(u, v)$ as

$$
R(u, v) = \iint_{\Omega} I(\xi, \eta) g(u - \xi, v - \eta)\, d\xi\, d\eta. \tag{5.5}
$$

**Table 5.1** Selection of the optimized Gabor features

(i) Give the test error rate for the $m$th sub-window by $(x_i, y_i)_{i=0}^N$, where $x_i$ is the parameter vector, $y_i$ is the error rate; $Y_0 = \{y_0, y_1, \ldots, y_N\}$. $P_0 = \{\}$;
(ii) Select the optimized filters
 For $t = 0, 1, 2, 3$
 Here: $index = \text{argmin}\|Y_t\|_\infty$
  $Y_t = Y_t - \{y_{\text{index}}\}$
  if $\|x_{\text{index}} - x_j\| > \epsilon, x_j \in P_t$
   then $P_t = P_t + \{x_{\max_t}\}$
  else
   goto Here
(iii) Get the best Gabor filter bank for the $m$th sub-window.

Although a linear feature could be directly used to represent (5.21), few scholars use it. The general Gabor features include thresholded Gabor feature, Gabor-energy feature, Complex moment Gabor feature, and grating cell operator feature. In our approach, we adopt the complex moment features of a Gabor filter response as the feature vector of our classifier.

We select the filter parameters with the strongest response for a certain sub-window including a vehicle part, and use SVM as a performance estimation classifier. The test image is divided into 9 overlapping sub-windows, and the statistical Gabor features from the convolution between sub-window image patch and a Gabor filter, mean $\mu$, standard deviation $\theta$, and the skewness $\kappa$ represent the vehicle [14]. We optimize the SVM parameters for each of the 9 sub-windows, and test the resulting 9 classifiers for each sub-window using test examples. Then we record the average error rate. At last, for each sub-window, the 4 Gabor filters with the minimum average error rate are combined into a filter bank for extracting a feature vector (see Table 5.1).

Then the 9 sub-windows with 4 Gabor filters each make a feature vector of size 108,

$$[\mu_{11}, \theta_{11}, \kappa_{11}, \mu_{12}, \theta_{12}, \kappa_{12}, \ldots, \mu_{93}, \theta_{93}, \kappa_{93}, \mu_{94}, \theta_{94}, \kappa_{94}],$$

where $\mu_{ij}, \theta_{ij}, \kappa_{ij}$, are the mean, standard deviation, and skewness, respectively; $i$ is the number of a sub-window, $j$ is the number of a filter.

## 5.5.2 SVM Classifier

SVM is an efficient approach to find the optimal hyperplane in a binary classification [3, 6, 17]. Here, the hyperplane has the maximum margin between two distinguished classes, which ensures not only the minimum empirical risk, but also the minimum Vapnik–Chervonenkis (VC) confidence.

Let $\{x_i, y_i\}$, $i = 0, 1, \ldots, L-1$, $y_i \in \{-1, 1\}$, $x_i \in \mathbb{R}^D$, be training samples. Assume that the hyperplane separates the positive samples from the negative ones.

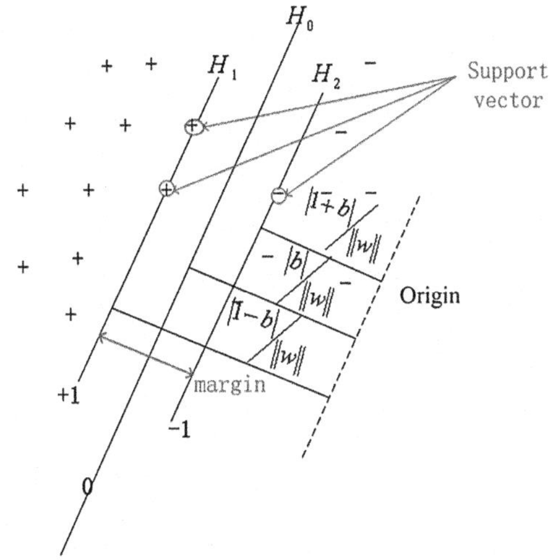


**Fig. 5.6** An illustration of a max margin classifier and support vector

Then, the point $x$ in the hyperplane satisfies

$$wx + b = 0, \tag{5.6}$$

where $w$ is the normal to the hyperplane, and $\frac{\|b\|}{\|w\|}$ is the distance from the origin to the hyperplane. For refine the margin of a separating hyperplane to be the shortest distance between the closest positive and negative sample, respectively, and the hyperplane. For the linearly separable case, the support vector machine seeks the hyperplane with the largest margin. Therefore, all training data should satisfy the following constraints

$$y_i(x_i w + b) - 1 \geq 0, \quad \forall i. \tag{5.7}$$

Now we consider two different types of points. For the points on the hyperplane $H_1$, we have

$$x_i w + b = 1. \tag{5.8}$$

Similarly, the points on the hyperplane $H_2$ satisfy the following equation

$$x_i w + b = -1. \tag{5.9}$$

The margin between $H_1$ and $H_2$ is

$$\text{margin} = \left| \frac{\|1+b\|}{\|w\|} - \frac{\|b\|}{\|w\|} \right| + \left| \frac{\|1-b\|}{\|w\|} - \frac{\|b\|}{\|w\|} \right| = 2\|w\|. \tag{5.10}$$

Thus we can obtain the optimal hyperplanes by minimizing $\|w\|^2$, resulting in the maximum margin classifiers. Moreover, define those training points on the hyperplanes $H_1$ and $H_2$ to be the support vectors, where the hyperplane $H_2$ is determined as shown in Fig. 5.6 using the extra circles.

Now we introduce unconstrained Lagrangian multipliers of the problem:

$$L_P = \frac{1}{2}\|w\|^2 - \sum_{i=0}^{L-1} \alpha_i y_i (x_i w + b) + \sum_{i=0}^{L-1} \alpha_i. \tag{5.11}$$

Minimizing $L_P$ w.r.t. $w$, $b$, $x_i$, we have

$$\begin{cases} w = \sum \alpha_i y_i x_i, \\ \sum_{i=0}^{L-1} \alpha_i y_i = 0. \end{cases} \tag{5.12}$$

Substituting (5.12) into (5.11), we have

$$L_D = \sum_{i=0}^{L-1} \alpha_i - \frac{1}{2} \sum_{i=0}^{L-1} \sum_{j=0}^{L-1} \alpha_i \alpha_j y_i y_j x_i x_j. \tag{5.13}$$

Note that $L_P$ in (5.11) and $L_D$ in (5.13) have the same objective function but with different constraints [3]. For the linearly separable case, we can obtain support vectors from (5.13) by maximizing $L_D$ w.r.t. $x_i$. In the solution, the points with $x_i > 0$ are the support vectors which determine the hyperplane. Finally, we obtain $w$ and $b$ from (5.12) and (5.6).

We will discuss the non-separable SVM. To make the method flexible, the inner products in (5.13) can be substituted by a kernel function $K[x_i, x_j]$. Thus, we have

$$L_D = \sum_{i=0}^{L-1} \alpha_i - \frac{1}{2} \sum_{i=0}^{L-1} \sum_{j=0}^{L-1} \alpha_i \alpha_j y_i y_j K[x_i, x_j]. \tag{5.14}$$

Kernel choice: There are many kernels investigated for computer vision and pattern recognition and they are as follows:

Polynomial Kernel:

$$K[x_i, x_j] = (x_i x_j + 1)^p. \tag{5.15}$$

RBF Kernel:

$$K[x_i, x_j] = e^{-\frac{\|x_i - x_j\|^2}{2\sigma^2}}, \tag{5.16}$$

Sigmoid Kernel:

$$K[x_i, x_j] = \tanh(k x_i y_i - \delta). \tag{5.17}$$

We use Radial Basis Functions as Kernel Functions.

If the training examples from two classes cause the two classes' margin to be maximal, then the classification hyperplane satisfies the following constrains:

$$f(x) = \sum_{i=1}^{L} y_i a_i k[x, x_i] + b, \tag{5.18}$$

**Fig. 5.7** The XJT AI&R vehicle examples database (the *left two images*) and the false examples of our detector (the *right two images*)

where $x, x_i \in \mathbb{R}^N$ are $N$-dimensional input feature vectors, $L$ is the number of labeled examples, $y_i \in (-1, 1)$ is the $i$th labeled example, and $k[x, x_i]$ is the inner product function. We use the radial basis function as a kernel function. For training the classifier, we selected 500 images from our vehicle database which was collected in Xi'an in 2005. They contain 1020 positive examples and 1020 negative examples. When testing the classifier, we get above 90% average right detection rate using 500 negative and positive examples independent of the training examples, and the missing and error detection rate is below 10%. Figure 5.7 shows the database, some false positive examples, and some false negative examples; Fig. 5.9 describes the ROC curve of the classifier.

## 5.6 Boosted Gabor Features

To reduce the computational burden and improve the performance in vehicle detection, we propose a supervised learning approach based on boosted Gabor features. A similar attempt to select the Gabor features is described in [13]. However, the choosen Gabor feature set in that study is larger than those in our study; moreover, the SVM is only used to classify objects during the period of recognizing step rather than the previous training step. Their approach may result in performance deterioration. In contrast, we use SVM as a classifier during the period of both the training step and classifying step.

## 5.6.1 Boosted Gabor Features Using AdaBoost

### 5.6.1.1 Gabor Feature

We first introduce some necessary definitions for Gabor filters and basic concepts for vehicle representation. The 2D Gabor function can be defined as follows:

$$G_p(u,v) = \frac{1}{2\pi\sigma_u\sigma_v} e^{-\frac{1}{2}(\frac{U^2}{\sigma_u^2}+\frac{V^2}{\sigma_v^2})} \cdot e^{2\pi j \hat{f} U}, \tag{5.19}$$

where

$$\begin{cases} U = (u,v)(\cos\varphi, \sin\varphi), \\ V = (-u,v)(\sin\varphi, \cos\varphi), \end{cases} \tag{5.20}$$

and $\hat{f}$ is the radius frequency of a complex sinusoidal signal modulating Gaussian function, $\varphi$ is the direction of a Gabor filter, $\sigma_u$ and $\sigma_v$ are the scale parameters of the filter, and $p = (\hat{f}, \varphi, \sigma_u, \sigma_v) \in \mathbb{R}^4$ represents all the parameters of a Gabor filter. Clearly, for image pixel set $\Omega$, Gabor features can be obtained by convolving the input image $I(u,v)$ $((u,v) \in \Omega)$ and a 2D Gabor filter $g(u,v)$ as

$$R(u,v) = \iint_{\Omega} I(\xi,\eta) g(u-\xi, v-\eta)\, d\xi\, d\eta. \tag{5.21}$$

Although a linear feature could be directly used to represent an object, few scholars do that. The most often used Gabor features are thresholded Gabor features, Gabor-energy features, Complex moment Gabor features, and grating cell operator features. In our approach, we adopt the complex moment features of a Gabor filter response as the feature vector of our classifier.

### 5.6.1.2 Boosted Gabor Features

The selection of different Gabor features has some effect on detection performance; however, the primary reason of selecting a Gabor filter is to find the Gabor filters strongly responding to the object of interest. The filter parameters are adjusted to obtain the strongest response for sub-windows comprising a vehicle part. The image is divided into 9 overlapping sub-windows, and the vehicle is represented with statistical features, mean $\mu$, standard deviation $\theta$, and the skewness $\kappa$, from a convolution between a sub-window and a Gabor filter [15].

**Table 5.2** BGF algorithm description

**Input**:
Training examples 1 $(I_i, y_i), 1 \leq i \leq n$; Training examples 2 $(I_j, y_j), n+1 \leq j \leq n+m$;
Gabor filters: $c_1, \ldots, c_N$; $y_i$ is the $i$th label of an example
**Computation**:
For each sub-window $s$
  For each Gabor filter $c$
    For each training example $(I_i, y_i)$
      $r(I_i, c; s) = (I_i \cap s) * c, \ i = 1, \ldots, n$
      Train the SVM classifier using the features
    For each training example $(I_j, y_j)$
      $r(I_j, c; s) = (I_j \cap s) * c, \ j = n+1, \ldots, n+m$
        Classify the training examples 2
  Do T times
    Obtain one feature using AdaBoost algorithm;
**Output**:
The 4 Gabor filters after 4 iterations with weights $\alpha_{i,j}$ for each sub-window.

Having obtained Gabor features of an object, it is time to evaluate the performance of a Gabor feature. Boosting approaches aim at improving the accuracy of any given learning algorithm and focusing on "difficult" examples. The AdaBoost algorithm proposed by E. Schapire is one of the most popular variations of basic boosting algorithms [7]. In its original form, it is used to improve the accuracy of any given learning algorithm. In our approach, it is used to boost the Gabor features for vehicle detection.

There are many Gabor features associated with a sub-window; however, few Gabor features are crucial for vehicle detection. Consequently, feature selection must be performed on these Gabor features. In our approach, we optimize the SVM classifier parameters for each of the 9 sub-windows, and then test the resulting 9 classifiers for each sub-window using test examples recording the classification rate of each Gabor filter for the 9 different sub-windows. According to the results, we perform the boosting task on a larger set of Gabor features using the AdaBoost algorithm, where each round of boosting finds one Gabor feature for a sub-window from the candidate features. After $T$ iterations, it yields $T$ Gabor filters for each sub-window (see Table 5.2). In our experiments, a total of 36 filters were combined into a feature vector to represent vehicles. The detection performance of BGF approach using the features after 4 iterations is better than those after 6 iterations.

The selection of a Gabor filter is to find the optimal parameter set in Gabor parameter space $\mathbb{R}^4$

$$\{p_1, \ldots, p_i, \ldots, p_N\},$$

where $p_i = (\hat{f}_i, \varphi_i, \sigma_{ui}, \sigma_{vi})$, and $N$ is the number of Gabor filters. For convenience of computing Gabor parameters are discretized. We define the range of $\hat{f}$ to be

$[\hat{f}_{\min}, \hat{f}_{\max}]$. According to the Nyquist theorem, the digital frequency $\omega = \pi$ corresponds to the maximum frequency of a band limited signal, and the frequencies higher than $\pi$ will be distorted. We write $\omega_{\max} = 2\pi f_{\max}/f_s = 2\pi \hat{f}_{\max}$, and then $\hat{f}_{\max} = \omega_{\max}/2\pi$, where $f$ is the general frequency, $f_s$ is the sampling frequency, and $\hat{f}_k$ is the $k$th normalized frequency that can be discretized by

$$\hat{f}_k = \hat{f}_{\min} + \frac{\hat{f}_{\max} - \hat{f}_{\min}}{L} a^k \quad \text{with } a = \left(\frac{\hat{f}_{\max}}{\hat{f}_{\min}}\right)^{\frac{1}{L-1}},$$

where $L$ is the number of sample points and $a$ is the sample scale. For the direction $\varphi$ of a filter, the filter response to an object in $[0, \pi]$ is the same as to an object in $[\pi, 2\pi]$.

The sample interval for uniform sampling is $\Delta\varphi = 180/P$ degrees, where $P$ is the number of samples for $\varphi$. The scale parameters $\sigma_x$ and $\sigma_y$ are actually the effective size of a Gaussian function, and their ranges are equal, say $[\sigma_{\min}, \sigma_{\max}]$. The upper limit $\sigma_{\max} = W_s/5$, where $W_s$ is the sub-window width, resulting in 98.7% energy in the range $[-\pi, \pi]$ of $\varphi$. At the same time, the lower limit $\sigma_{\min}$ equals 0, and the number of samples for both $\sigma_x$ and $\sigma_y$ is $M$.

In the experiments of our approach, $a = 1.5588$, $L = 15$, $P = 15$, $M = 10$, $N = 22500$, $W_s = 40$, $\hat{f} \in [\hat{f}_{\min}, \hat{f}_{\max}] = [0, 0.5]$, and $\sigma_x, \sigma_y \in = [0, 8]$. Figure 5.8 shows our boosted Gabor filters for vehicle detection.

## 5.6.2 *Experimental Results and Analysis*

### 5.6.2.1 Vehicle Database for Detection and Tracking

For vehicle detection and tracking, we collected the vehicle video database under two conditions: general and hard ones. According to weather, daytime, road type, and congestion, we collected images of several kinds of vehicles, such as sedans, trucks, and motorcycles. The host vehicle collecting the video operated at 3 different speeds: 40, 80, and 120 km/h. Table 5.3 is the summary of various road conditions for video collection, and here $*$ indicates hard conditions; $\surd$ indicates general conditions.

### 5.6.2.2 Boosted Gabor Features

We have carried out vehicle detection using, apart from our approach, the EGFO approach and a no-boosting approach. The distribution of Gabor filter parameters $(\hat{f}, \varphi, \sigma_x, \sigma_y)$ is shown in Fig. 5.10. We can see that our boosted Gabor filters are different from the optimized Gabor filters using EGFO because each Gabor filter in our approach is optimized for a sub-window rather than for a complete image. For the frequency of Gabor filters, the boosted filters tend to have a low frequency due

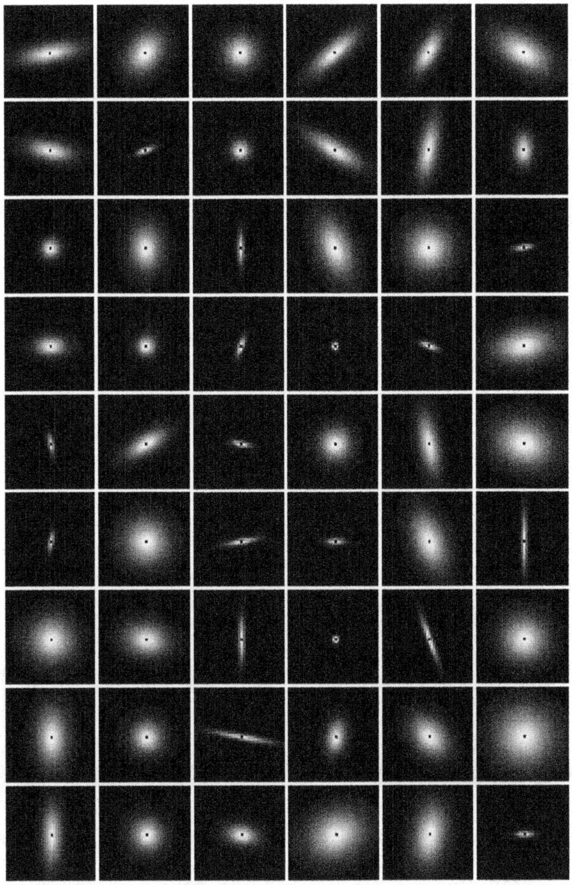

**Fig. 5.8** Boosted Gabor filters using AdaBoost algorithm: each row shows the boosted Gabor filters for one sub-window, and the $i$th column represents the Gabor filter after the $i$th iteration

**Table 5.3** The collection conditions of vehicle video

| Conditions | Curve | Straight | Upslope |
|---|---|---|---|
| No traffic congestion | * | * | * |
| Traffic congestion | | √ | |
| Sunny | * | * | * |
| Cloudy | * | * | * |
| Rain | √ | √ | √ |
| After rain | √ | √ | √ |
| Against sun | | √ | √ |
| Night | √ | √ | √ |

to large structures in vehicles, like windows and bumpers. The directions of most of the boosted Gabor filters are close to 0°, 45°, 90°, and 135° (see the second subfigure of Fig. 5.10), due to the prevalence of these angles in vehicles. In addition,

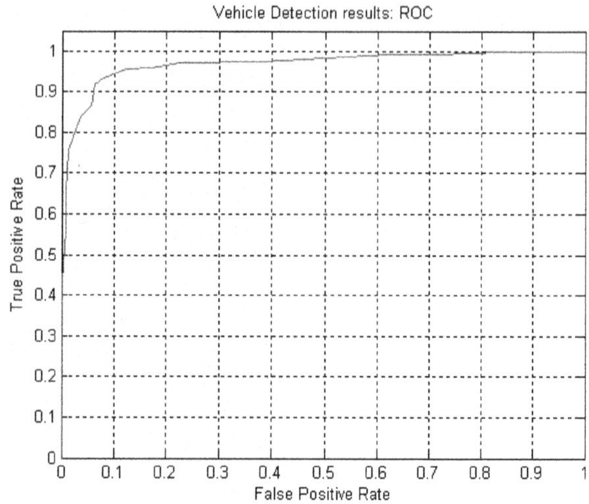


**Fig. 5.9** ROC curves for our vehicle classifier

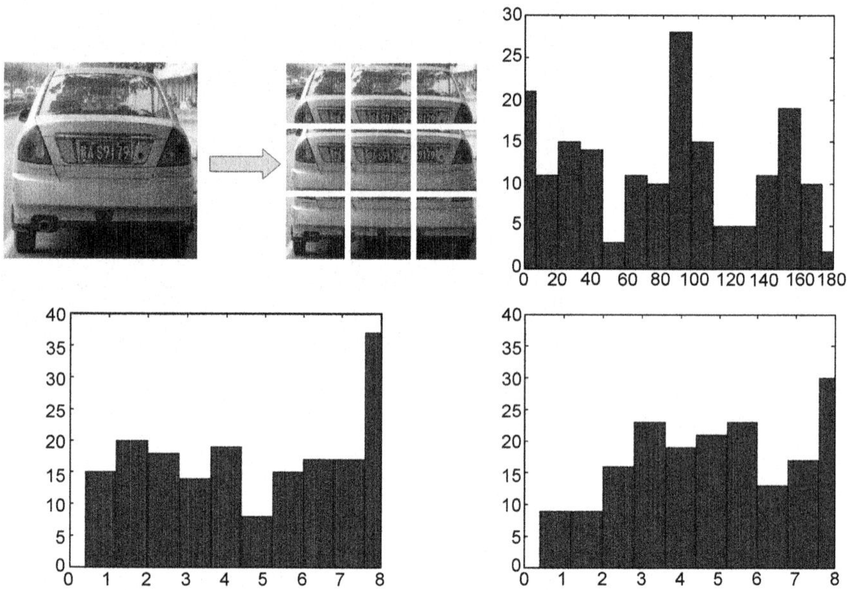


**Fig. 5.10** The distribution of the parameters of Gabor Filters

from the latter two sub-figures of Fig. 5.10, it follows that $\sigma_y$ is larger than $\sigma_x$, in accordance with vehicles being wider rather than higher. To summarize, the choice of Gabor filter parameters is heavily dependent on the detection object, a Gabor filter that works well for vehicles probably does not work for pedestrians, and vice versa. Our Gabor filter selection optimized for vehicle detection results in better performance than those based on previous selection methods (Fig. 5.11). For training the classifier, we selected 500 images from our vehicle database which was collected in

Fig. 5.11 Vehicle detection based on hypothesis validation

Xi'an in 2005. They contain 1020 positive examples and 1020 negative examples. In testing the classifier, we use 500 negative and positive examples independent of the training examples.

For the validation of the performance of our BGF approach, the vehicle detection experiments were performed on three different optimization approaches for 22,500 Gabor filters. The experimental results show the Average Right Rate (ARR) of a no-boosting Gabor feature approach to be 90%, that of BGF approach to be 96%, and that of EGFO approach to be 91%. Figure 5.12(a) is the comparison of our detector with the other two approaches, and the Receiver Operating Characteristics (ROC) curves that compare different boosting approaches are shown in Fig. 5.9. These figures show that our vehicle detector has good discrimination ability with a low decision bias when comparing the no-boosting and EGFO algorithms.

#### 5.6.2.3 Vehicle Detection Results and Discussions

We tested our vehicle detector on the collected video using the Springrobot platform [10]. Figures 5.13 and 5.14 show the results of our vehicle detector under general and hard conditions, respectively. We proposed an approach for vehicle classification and detection with good time performance using vanishing points and ROIs and achieving high detection accuracy using Gabor features. The method using the vanishing point to define ROIs eliminates the disturbing effects of some non-vehicle objects, improving both the detection rate and the robustness of this approach. The detection speed of our vehicle detector is approximately 20 frames/second on a Pentium® 4 CPU 2.4 GHz both for the general and hard conditions. The detection rate is defined by

$$r = \frac{\sum_{i=1}^{N}(nt_i - nf_i)}{\sum_{j=1}^{N}(nv_j)}, \tag{5.22}$$

**Fig. 5.12** Two kinds of curves comparing different Gabor filter optimization approaches

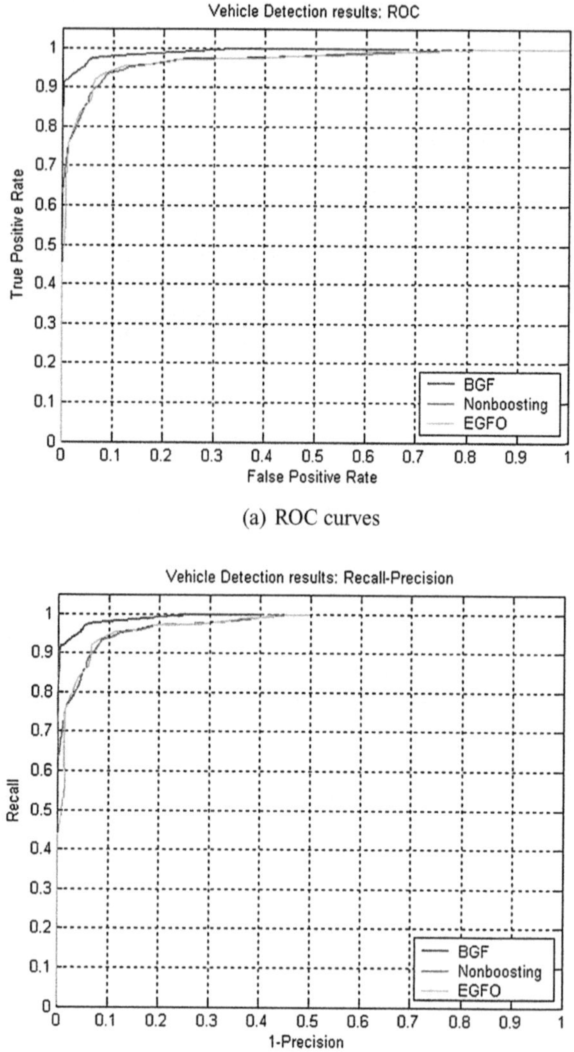


(a) ROC curves

(b) Recall-precision curves

where $nt_i$ represents the number of right detection in the $i$th frame; $nf_i$ represents the error detection rate in the $i$th frame; $nv_j$ represents the actual number of vehicles in the $j$th frame. With this definition, our vehicle detection rate is above 90%.

In our approach, we have introduced a structure of hypothesis and validation for vehicle classification and detection. The experimental results of our system so far show that the algorithm works well on a structured road. Extension of this approach to unstructured roads needs to be investigated. Additionally, under the conditions of congestion, the constraints are too strong to detect all vehicles but the unobstructed vehicles are all detected. Further research work will focus on these problems.

**Fig. 5.13** Vehicle detection results under the general conditions

**Fig. 5.14** Vehicle detection results under the hard conditions

## References


1. Autio, I., Elomaa, T.: Flexible view recognition for indoor navigation based on Gabor filters and support vector machines. Pattern Recognit. **36**(12), 2769–2779 (2003)
2. Broggi, A., Cerri, P., Antonello, P.: Multi-resolution vehicle detection using artificial vision. In: IEEE Intelligent Vehicle Symposium, pp. 310–314 (2004)
3. Burges, C.: A tutorial on support vector machines for pattern recognition. Data Min. Knowl. Discov. **2**(2), 121–167 (1998)
4. Cheng, H., Zheng, N., Sun, C., van de Wetering, H.: Vanishing point and Gabor feature based multi-resolution on-road vehicle detection. In: International Symposium on Neural Networks, pp. 46–51 (2006)
5. Du, Y., Papanikolopoulos, N.: Real-time vehicle following through a novel symmetry-based approach IEEE Int. Conf. Robot. Autom. **4**, 3160–3165 (1997)
6. Duda, R., Hart, P., Stork, D.: Pattern Classification. CiteSeer, Princeton (2001)
7. Freund, Y., Schapire, R.: A desicion-theoretic generalization of on-line learning and an application to boosting. In: Computational Learning Theory. Springer, Berlin (1995)
8. Lampert, C., Blaschko, M., Hofmann, T.: Beyond sliding windows: Object localization by efficient subwindow search. In: IEEE Conference on Computer Vision and Pattern Recognition (2008)
9. Leibe, B., Cornelis, N., Cornelis, K., Van Gool, L.: Dynamic 3D scene analysis from a moving vehicle. In: IEEE Conference on Computer Vision and Pattern Recognition (2007)
10. Li, Q., Zheng, N., Cheng, H.: Springrobot: A prototype autonomous vehicle and its algorithms for lane detection. IEEE Trans. Intell. Transp. Syst. **5**(4), 300–308 (2004)
11. Liu, T., Zheng, N., Zhao, L., Cheng, H.: Learning based symmetric features selection for vehicle detection. In: IEEE International Symposium on Intelligent Vehicle, pp. 124–129 (2005)
12. Manjunath, B., Ma, W.: Texture features for browsing and retrieval of image data. IEEE Trans. Pattern Anal. Mach. Intell. **18**(8), 837–842 (1996)
13. Shen, L., Bai, L.: Adaboost gabor feature selection for classification. In: Proc. of Image and Vision Computing, pp. 77–83 (2004)

14. Sun, Z., Bebis, G., Miller, R.: On-road vehicle detection using evolutionary gabor filter optimization. IEEE Trans. Intell. Transp. Syst. **6**(2), 125–137 (2005)
15. Sun, Z., Bebis, G., Miller, R.: On-road vehicle detection using evolutionary Gabor filter optimization. IEEE Trans. Intell. Transp. Syst. **6**, 125–137 (2005)
16. Tsai, D., Wu, S., Chen, M.: Optimal Gabor filter design for texture segmentation using stochastic optimization. Image Vis. Comput. **19**(5), 299–316 (2001)
17. Vapnik, V.: The Nature of Statistical Learning Theory. Springer, Berlin (2000)
18. Weldon, T., Higgins, W., Dunn, D.: Efficient Gabor filter design for texture segmentation. Pattern Recognit. **29**(12), 2005–2015 (1996)
19. Zhang, L., Li, S., Qu, Z., Huang, X.: Boosting local feature based classifiers for face recognition. In: The first IEEE workshop on Face Processing in Video, p. 87 (2004)
20. Zheng, N., Tang, S., Cheng, H., Li, Q., Lai, G., Wang, F.: Toward intelligent driver-assistance and safety warning system. IEEE Intell. Syst. **19**(2), 8–11 (2004)

# Chapter 6
# Multiple-Sensor Based Multiple-Object Tracking

## 6.1 Introduction

As we mentioned in previous chapters, vision sensors are capable of estimating the relative position between the host vehicle and other vehicles, determining the shapes of obstacles and lanes. However, vision sensors could depend on weather and lighting conditions. Moreover, using single vision sensors it is difficult to estimate the longitudinal distance since perspective projections remove depth information. A radar/lidar based system is robust to weather and lighting conditions, and it is also easy to estimate depth information. In conclusion, radar/lidar and vision sensors have complementary properties. The systems combining these sensors remarkably improve overall system performance.

## 6.2 Related Work

Multi-sensor multi-object detection and tracking systems have received considerable attention over the last 5 years [1, 5, 6, 9–11, 14, 15, 17, 18]. In [17], a strategy that distinguishes between a static object and a moving object by estimating object speed has been proposed, where both the speed and the direction of the objects and the host vehicle are used to estimate the speed. In [9], three different geometric object models are designed for small objects, the objects described by a rectangular shape like that of a car, and free-form objects, respectively. In terms of obstacle classification and tracking, the most generally used combination approach consists of a camera and a range sensor [1, 9, 11, 17]. An approach that simplifies the fusion between range and vision sensors using corresponding sets of hypothesis was proposed in [1]. In this system, a radar device and a monocular camera are fused by sharing sets of hypotheses for the detection of vehicles. In [5], a decentralized multiple-sensor multiple-target tracking approach for the Autotaxi system is considered for avoiding collisions, where the tracking involves three stages: data alignment, track-to-track association, and track fusion. A sensor fusion strategy that introduces depth

H. Cheng, *Autonomous Intelligent Vehicles*,
Advances in Computer Vision and Pattern Recognition,
DOI 10.1007/978-1-4471-2280-7_6, 

cue into the segmentation algorithm improves the target segmentation performance due to the complement of radar and vision [6]. As a pre-crash system, SAVE-U project aims at protecting pedestrians and bicyclists and avoiding collisions between pedestrians and vehicles, where the sensor platform consists of radar sensors, normal cameras, and infrared cameras. Alternatively, another combination form, such as using an infrared camera and a radar [14], has good performance in driver assistance systems.

In environment perception, CHAUFFEUR Assistant system combined both radar and video sensors, providing vehicle controllers with valuable data about preceding vehicles and about the lane.

In Highway Lane Change Assistant (HLCA), vision and radar sensors are combined to detect dangerous objects in the neighboring lanes [16], which was evaluated by different drivers in different vehicles. On German highways, the common vision-based lane recognition system is proved to be affected by weather, a fusion approach was used to estimated road structures and the positions of the other vehicles in front by combining vision and radar sensors [7]. Combining radar-based ACC and visional perception, a Hybrid Adaptive Cruise Control (HACC) was created to first detect and track lanes and vehicles. And afterwards this information was used in the longitudinal controllers [8].

## 6.3 Obstacles Stationary or Moving Judgement Using Lidar Data

A lidar sensor is often used as an on-board sensor for driver assistance systems. Much effort about clustering the original data and classifying the objects using a lidar sensor have been made [13, 17]. A method consisting of three modules: scan segmentation, object classification, and object tracking by a lidar is used to detect and track multiple objects [13]. A strategy is proposed for distinguishing all objects detected by a lidar and for dividing them into three categories: moving objects, roadside reflectors, and overhead sign [17], where the motion of detected objects is judged by the relationship between the path of the host vehicle and changes in the positions of the objects. The position and size of obstacles are not sufficient to assess its safety in $I^2$DASW systems, and the various behaviors of all the obstacles on the road should also be considered, such as the velocity and the acceleration. We have developed an algorithm to estimate the velocity of all obstacles.

First, we segment the lidar data into several clusters, and each cluster represents one target. According to the distance between two laser points, we can judge whether two points belong to an object or not by the following equation [13]

$$r_{k,k+1} \le r_{\min} \frac{2\tan\beta \sin(\frac{\phi}{2})}{\cos(\frac{\phi}{2}) - \sin(\frac{\phi}{2})\tan\beta}, \tag{6.1}$$

where $r_k$ is the distance of the $k$th point to the laser device, $r_{k,k+1} = |r_k - r_{k+1}|$, $r_{\min} = \min\{r_k, r_{k+1}\}$, $\phi$ is the angular resolution. In our experiments, $\phi = 0.25°$ and $\beta = 85°$.

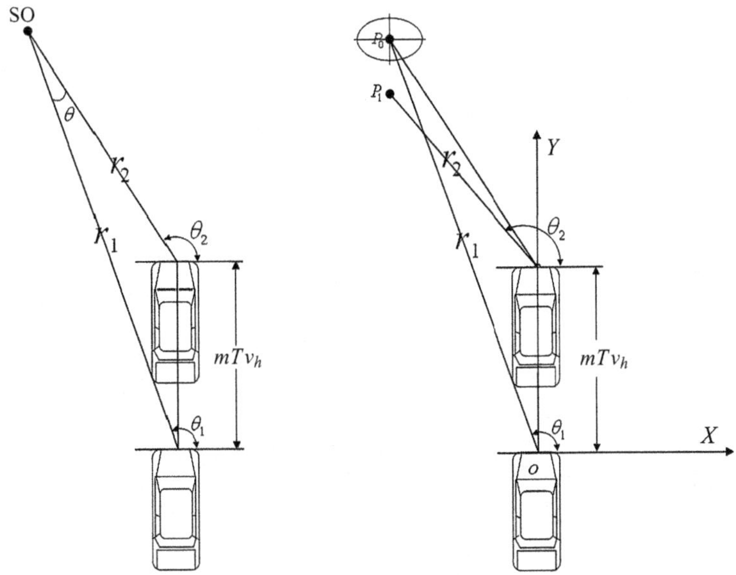


(a) Host vehicle velocity computation.

(b) Moving object velocity computation.

**Fig. 6.1** Our velocity estimation approach

In many similar systems, the vehicle speed is measured by the encoder [2]. In contrast, we proposed a vehicle speed estimation algorithm by using a static object given the two observation values $(r_1, \theta_1)$ and $(r_2, \theta_2)$ as follows:

$$v_h = \left[r_1^2 + r_2^2 - 2r_1 r_2 \cos(\theta_1 - \theta_2)\right]/(mT), \tag{6.2}$$

where $T$ is the sampling interval; $m$ is the number of the consecutive frames, and it is generally larger than 1 for improving the velocity accuracy. Here we assume that over a small interval of time $mT$ the driving direction of the host vehicle is consistent with the $Y$-axis in the Cartesian coordinates system $XOY$ as shown in Fig. 6.1. After finishing the velocity estimation of a host vehicle, we can obtain the coordinates of two segments: $P_0 = (x_0, y_0)$ and $P_1 = (x_1, y_1)$. Therefore,

$$x_0 = -r_1 \cos\theta_1, \qquad y_0 = r_1 \sin\theta_1, \tag{6.3}$$

$$x_1 = -r_2 \cos\theta_2, \qquad y_1 = x_2 m T v_h + r_2 \sin\theta_2. \tag{6.4}$$

Then we can estimate the absolute velocity of stable objects in the scene by the following equation

$$v_o = \frac{\sqrt{(y_1 - y_0)^2 + (x_1 - x_0)^2}}{mT}. \tag{6.5}$$

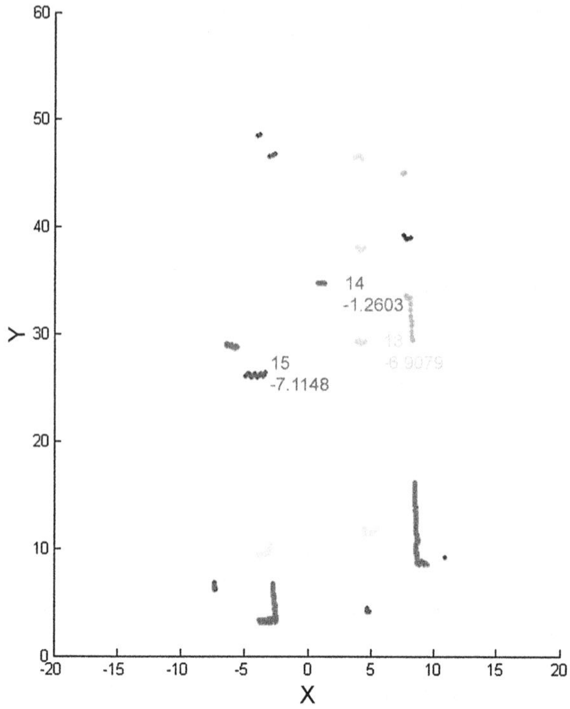


**Fig. 6.2** Lidar clustering and speed estimation

Considering the noise and vibration of the lidar, we can judge whether an object is moving or is stationary by the Mahalanobis distance given two segments $P_0$ and $P_1$:

$$d = (P_0 - P_1)^T \Sigma^{-1}(P_0 - P_1),$$

where $\Sigma$ is a covariance matrix reflecting the uncertainty characteristics of lidar data. If $d < d_0$, the object is stationary, otherwise the object is moving. Here the decision rule can be interpreted geometrically as saying that the distance between the two points is less than $d_0$, taking into account the variance. Figure 6.2 shows the results of velocity estimation using our algorithm, where the 13th, 14th and 15th objects are stable for several consecutive frames.

## 6.4 Multi-obstacle Tracking and Situation Assessment

### *6.4.1 Multi-obstacle Tracking Based on EKF Using a Single Sensor*

#### 6.4.1.1 Probability Framework of Tracking

From the viewpoint of probability, tracking is a kind of statistical inference, in other words, given the observation values at time 1 and extending up to and including time

$k$: $Z_{1:k} = \{z_1, z_2, \ldots, z_k\}$, we may construct the posterior probability $P(X_k|Z_{1:k})$, and then obtain the estimate $\hat{X}_k$ and the covariance matrix $P$ of the state vector $X_k$ at time $k$.

For the sake of simplicity, we make two assumptions:

1. The state at the current time $k$ only depends on the state at the last time $k-1$, which is called a first order Markov Process. Consequently, it yields the following equation

$$P(X_k|X_{k-1}, X_{k-2}, \ldots) = P(X_k|X_{k-1}).$$

2. The observation at current time $k$ depends only on the current state $P(Z_{1:k}|X_k) = P(Z_k|X_k)P(Z_{1:k-1}|X_k)$.

By hypothesis, we can deduce the Bayesian posterior probability

$$P(X_k|Z_{1:k}) = \frac{P(Z_k|X_k)P(X_k|Z_{1:k-1})}{P(Z_{1:k}|Z_{1:k-1})}, \tag{6.6}$$

where $P(X_k|Z_{1:k})$ is the posterior probability, $P(Z_k|X_k)$ is the likelihood, $P(X_k|Z_{1:k-1})$ is the prior probability, and $P(Z_{1:k}|Z_{1:k-1}) = \int P(Z_k|X_k)P(X_k|Z_{1:k-1})dX_k$ is the belief.

For the probability framework of a tracking problem, we may proceed in the manner described next:

3. Prediction Step. Given $P(X_{k-1}|Z_{1:k-1})$, we can obtain $P(X_k|Z_{1:k-1})$ and $\hat{X}_{k|k-1}$.
4. Update Step. Given $P(X_{k-1}|Z_{1:k-1})$ and $Z_k$, we can obtain $P(X_k|Z_{1:k})$ and $\hat{X}_{k|k}$.

#### 6.4.1.2 System Model

In this system, we adopt the constant acceleration model to build the system equation

$$\begin{cases} X_k = FX_{k-1} + G \cdot v, \\ Z_k = h(X_k) + w. \end{cases} \tag{6.7}$$

The state vector at time $k$ defined as

$$X_k = [x_k, \dot{x}_k, \ddot{x}_k, y_k, \dot{y}_k, \ddot{y}_k]^T,$$

where $x_k, \dot{x}_k, \ddot{x}_k$ are the position, velocity, and acceleration in the $x$-direction at time $k$; $y_k, \dot{y}_k, \ddot{y}_k$ are the position, velocity, and acceleration in the $y$-direction at time $k$.

The state transition matrix can be written as

$$F = \begin{bmatrix} 1 & T & T^2/2 & 0 & 0 & 0 \\ 0 & 1 & T & 0 & 0 & 0 \\ 0 & 0 & 1 & 0 & 0 & 0 \\ 0 & 0 & 0 & 1 & T & T^2/2 \\ 0 & 0 & 0 & 0 & 1 & T \\ 0 & 0 & 0 & 0 & 0 & 1 \end{bmatrix}, \tag{6.8}$$

where $T$ is the sampling interval of a sensor. In (6.7), $\upsilon = [\upsilon_{a_x}, \upsilon_{a_y}]^T$ is process noise, modeled as a zero-mean white noise whose correlation matrix is defined by

$$E\{\upsilon_k \upsilon_j^T\} = \begin{bmatrix} \sigma_x^2 & 0 \\ 0 & \sigma_y^2 \end{bmatrix} \delta_{kj},$$

where $n$ is the dimension of $\upsilon$; and here $n = 2$. The process noise distribution matrix corresponding to the above is

$$G = \begin{bmatrix} T^2/2 & 0 \\ T & 0 \\ 1 & 0 \\ 0 & T^2/2 \\ 0 & T \\ 0 & 1 \end{bmatrix}. \tag{6.9}$$

We define the observation value at time $k$ as

$$Z_k = \begin{bmatrix} r_k \\ \theta_k \end{bmatrix}, \tag{6.10}$$

and its observation function is

$$h(x_k) = \begin{bmatrix} \sqrt{x_k^2 + y_k^2} \\ tg^{-1}[y_k/x_k] \end{bmatrix}. \tag{6.11}$$

Therefore, we can get the following form

$$\begin{cases} x_k = r_k \cos(\theta_k), \\ y_k = r_k \sin(\theta_k). \end{cases} \tag{6.12}$$

In this system, the states of objects are in the Cartesian coordinate system, while observation values are in the polar coordinate system. Consequently, the observation equation is nonlinear. We may now linearize $h(X)$ around $X = \hat{X}_{k|k-1}$ and obtain the observation matrix

$$H_k = \left.\frac{\partial h}{\partial X}\right|_{X=\hat{X}_{k|k-1}} = \begin{bmatrix} \frac{\hat{x}_{k|k-1}}{\sqrt{\hat{x}_{k|k-1}^2+\hat{y}_{k|k-1}^2}} & 0 & 0 & \frac{\hat{y}_{k|k-1}}{\sqrt{\hat{x}_{k|k-1}^2+\hat{y}_{k|k-1}^2}} & 0 & 0 \\ \frac{-\hat{y}_{k|k-1}}{\hat{x}_{k|k-1}^2+\hat{y}_{k|k-1}^2} & 0 & 0 & \frac{\hat{x}_{k|k-1}}{\hat{x}_{k|k-1}^2+\hat{y}_{k|k-1}^2} & 0 & 0 \end{bmatrix}. \tag{6.13}$$

In (6.7), $w = [w_r, w_\theta]$ is the observation noise, modeled as a zero-mean white noise whose correlation matrix is defined by

$$E\{w_k w_j^T\} = \begin{bmatrix} \sigma_r^2 & 0 \\ 0 & \sigma_\theta^2 \end{bmatrix} \delta_{kj} = R\delta_{kj},$$

where $n$ is the dimension of $w$; and here $n = 2$.

Combining the probability framework of tracking with the Minimum Mean Square Error (MMSE), we can obtain the EKF's prediction equation

$$\begin{cases} \hat{X}_{k|k-1} = F X_{k-1|k-1}, \\ P_{k|k-1} = F P_{k-1|k-1} F^T + G Q G^T, \end{cases} \tag{6.14}$$

where $\hat{X}_{k|k-1}$ is the state prediction at time $k$ given the state at time $k-1$ and $P(k|k-1)$ is the prediction covariance.

The update equation given $z_k$ and $\hat{X}_{k|k-1}$ at time $k$ can be written in the form

$$\begin{cases} \hat{X}_{k|k} = \hat{X}_{k|k-1} + W_k [Z_k - H_k \hat{X}_{k|k-1}], \\ P_{k|k} = P_{k|k-1} - W_k S W_k^T, \end{cases} \tag{6.15}$$

$$\begin{cases} S = H P_{k|k-1} H^T + R, \\ W_k = P_{k|k-1} H^T S^{-1}, \end{cases} \tag{6.16}$$

where $S$ is the observation prediction covariance, and $W_k$ is the Kalman gain, $\hat{X}_{k|k}$ is the output of state update, and $P_{k|k}$ is the update state covariance.

#### 6.4.1.3 Initial Conditions

Concerning the initialization of the EKF, we determine the local tracks by using the acceleration of three points where it is assumed that motion of an object is modeled as having constant acceleration, finishing the initialization operation; for details we refer to [15].

#### 6.4.1.4 Data Association for a Single Sensor

For lidar and radar data, data association is the first of all steps when new data arrive, aiming at judging the corresponding relation between the current observation and the previous track. Our data association includes two categories: observation-to-observation and observation-to-track. The main objective of the association between observations is to initialize tracks correctly, while the association between an observation and a track aims at holding and updating the existing tracks.

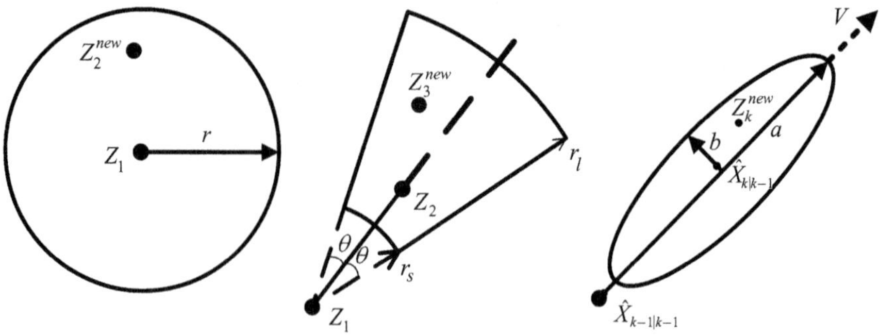


**Fig. 6.3** Various association gates: circle, sector, and ellipse

**1. Observation-to-Observation Association** When a new object appears, we can hold the observation directly. For a single point, we do not know the moving direction of the object. In that case, when the object has an observation $z_1$, we use the circle association gate to judge the correlation between $z_1$ and $z_2^{\text{new}}$ without a moving direction (see Fig. 6.3).

To associate a new observation, the next problem is to compute the radius of the association gate $r$. The radius of an associate gate is defined as

$$\Delta r_{\max} = (v_h - v_o) \cdot T_s, \tag{6.17}$$

where $v_h$ is the velocity of the host vehicle, $v_o$ is the velocity of the obstacle. If $|z_2^{\text{new}} - z_1| \leq \Delta r_{\max}$, it means that $z_2^{\text{new}}$ is correlated with $z_1$, otherwise they do not correlate (see Fig. 6.3).

If there are two existing observation points of a certain object, $z_1$ and $z_2$, we can use a sector association gate to judge the correlation between $z_3^{\text{new}}$ and $z_2$ (see Fig. 6.3). If the following inequality is satisfied

$$\begin{cases} r_s \leq |\overline{z_1 z_3^{\text{new}}}| \leq r_l, \\ |\arg(\overline{z_1 z_3^{\text{new}}}) - \arg(\overline{z_1 z_2})| \leq \theta, \end{cases} \tag{6.18}$$

then $z_3^{\text{new}}$ is located inside the association gate, which represents the correlation between $z_3^{\text{new}}$ and $z_2$. Here $\theta$ is a threshold value.

**2. Observation-to-Track Association** During the period of tracking, we obtain the state update value of a track $\hat{X}_{k-1|k-1}$ at time $k-1$ and the state prediction value of a track $\hat{X}_{k|k-1}$ at time $k$. Combining observation value $z_k^{\text{new}}$ at time $k$ with the previous two state values judges whether $z_k^{\text{new}}$ is associated with $\hat{X}_{k|k-1}$ or not.

After the initialization of tracks, it yields the state estimates of objects by using a prediction-and-update model. In general, the longer exiting period results in lesser estimation covariance. In our approach, we set an ellipse association gate with its center $\hat{X}_{k|k-1}$ (see Fig. 6.3), and choose the motion direction of an object as a major axis.

Define the new observation as

$$z_k^{\text{new}} = \left[r_k^{\text{new}}, \theta_k^{\text{new}}\right].$$

Consequently, we obtain the Cartesian coordinates of the observation given the observation value $z_k^{\text{new}}$ in the form

$$\begin{cases} x_k^{\text{new}} = r_k^{\text{new}} \cos(\theta_k^{\text{new}}), \\ y_k^{\text{new}} = r_k^{\text{new}} \sin(\theta_k^{\text{new}}). \end{cases} \tag{6.19}$$

Then we can obtain the state prediction value

$$\hat{X}_{k|k-1} = [x_{k|k-1},\ \dot{x}_{k|k-1},\ \ddot{x}_{k|k-1},\ y_{k|k-1},\ \dot{y}_{k|k-1},\ \ddot{y}_{k|k-1}]^T$$

and the motion direction of the object

$$\theta_o = \arctan\left(\frac{\dot{y}_{k|k-1}}{\dot{x}_{k|k-1}}\right).$$

Here $\theta_o$ is the rotation angle of the ellipse association gate.

On the basis of the previous results, we get the ellipse equation of the association gate

$$\frac{x_e^2}{a^2} + \frac{y_e^2}{b^2} = 1, \tag{6.20}$$

where

$$\begin{cases} x_e = (x - x_{k|k-1}) \cos\theta_o + (y - y_{k|k-1}) \sin\theta_o, \\ y_e = (x - x_{k|k-1})(-\sin\theta_o) + (y - y_{k|k-1}) \cos\theta_o. \end{cases} \tag{6.21}$$

We may now define a distance function

$$d_{X,Z} = \frac{x_e^2}{a^2} + \frac{y_e^2}{b^2}, \tag{6.22}$$

where $a$ and $b$ are the half-lengths of the two axes of an ellipse.

Substituting the observation value $z_k^{\text{new}} = (x_k^{\text{new}}, y_k^{\text{new}})$ into (6.22), $d_{X,Z} \le 1$ indicates that $z_k^{\text{new}}$ and $\hat{X}_{k|k-1}$ are correlated; while $d_{X,Z} > 1$ indicates that $z_k^{\text{new}}$ is uncorrelated with $\hat{X}_{k|k-1}$.

On the basis of the distance function of the above observation-to-observation and observation-to-track association, we build a distance matrix for all the passing points, and use Global Nearest Neighbor (GNN) algorithm to associate the observation with observation or a track.

#### 6.4.1.5 Single Track Management

A single track management is an important step of object tracking. In our approach, for every observation point, if there are 3 correlated observation values among 5 consecutive values, we can initialize the EKF, finishing the start of a track.

Track holding is to keep the tracks of objects continuously by the beforehand stated rules after the start of the tracks. We use a sliding window detector to hold tracks, where an $N/M$ rule is used to judge whether these tracks exist. In other words, $N$ correlated observation values out of $M$ observation values are considered for the track to exist. With the increase of the holding time of a track, the belief of this track is getting bigger and bigger. Consequently, in terms of actual implementation, $M$ and $N/M$ during the start period of a track can be set to a smaller value than that of the later period of tracking. In our approach, $M = 8$, $N = 5$.

To process a vanishing object, canceling of tracks is necessary. There are three categories tracks required to be canceled. The first one is the point without initialization: If there are no 3 correlated consecutive observation values, the track is canceled. The second one is a start track: If the $N/M$ rule is violated, the track is canceled. The third one is a track made by a reverse direction object: When the object moves behind a host car, the track can be canceled immediately. Figure 6.4 shows the tracks of multiple objects using a radar sensor.

### 6.4.2 Lidar and Radar Track Fusion

#### 6.4.2.1 Data Alignment

Since lidars and radars work independently and are unsynchronized, for multi-sensor fusion, we must first transform the different coordinates into the same coordinate system and then fuse the local tracks. Here we map the lidar coordinates and radar coordinates into the vehicle coordinates to solve the position alignment. Moreover, we synchronize time between lidar and radar by using the prediction equation of EKF.

#### 6.4.2.2 Track Association

On the basis of the two local tracks of a lidar and a radar, $\hat{X}_l$ and $\hat{X}_r$, we can yield the corresponding relation between the two local tracks. The distance function is defined as [3, 5]

$$d_{lr} = (\hat{X}_l - \hat{X}_r)^T (P_l + P_r - P_{lr} - P_{rl})^{-1} (\hat{X}_l - \hat{X}_r). \tag{6.23}$$

In actual implementation, we neglect the cross-covariance matrixes between the lidar and radar: $P_{lr}$ and $P_{rl}$, that is, $P_{lr} = P_{rl} = 0$.

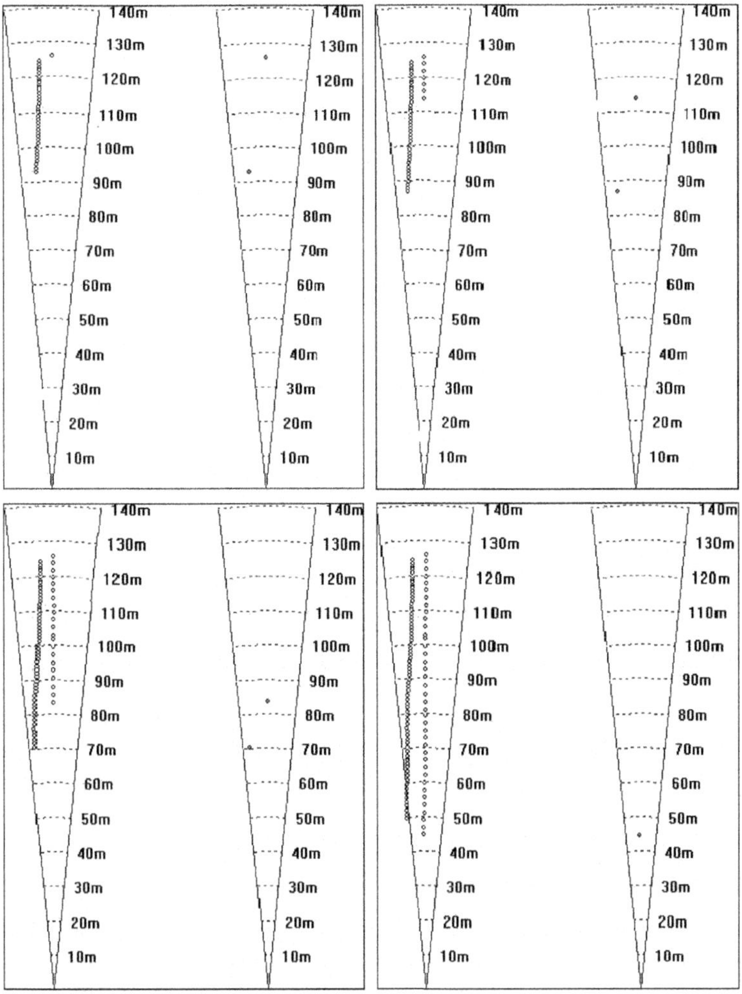


**Fig. 6.4** Multiple-object tracking using a radar sensor

Let $x = d_{ij}$, and suppose it has a $\chi^2$ distribution with $M$ degrees of freedom with the density in the form [3]

$$f(x) = \frac{1}{2^{\frac{M}{2}}\Gamma(\frac{M}{2})} x^{\frac{M-2}{2}} e^{-\frac{x}{2}}, \tag{6.24}$$

where $\Gamma$ is the Gamma function with the following properties:

$$\Gamma\left(\frac{1}{2}\right) = \sqrt{\pi}, \qquad \Gamma(1) = 1, \qquad \Gamma(m+1) = m\Gamma(m).$$

The probability of $x \in (0, \sigma)$ may be written as

$$\alpha = \int_0^{\sigma} f(x)\,dx.$$

On the basis of a $\sigma$ corresponding to a given $\alpha$, we can set the ellipse association gate

$$\begin{cases} H_0 : d_{lr} \le \sigma, \\ H_1 : d_{lr} > \sigma, \end{cases} \tag{6.25}$$

where $H_0$ indicates that $\hat{X}_l$ and $\hat{X}_r$ come from the same object; $H_1$ indicates that $\hat{X}_l$ and $\hat{X}_r$ come from two different objects.

Assumed that there are $N$ track pairs which pass the association gate, we rank the track pairs by the corresponding distance value $d_{ij}$. Since one object has only one track pair, we take the track pair with the minimum distance value $d_{lr}$.

#### 6.4.2.3 Track Fusion Algorithm

There now remains the problem of track fusion given local tracks of the lidar and radar, $\hat{X}_l$ and $\hat{X}_r$, and their covariance matrixes: $P_r$ and $P_l$. To solve track fusion, we use the Maximum Likelihood Estimation (MLE) approach to fuse the tracks [5]. First of all, we assume that the state estimation error has a Gaussian distribution, and then obtain the state estimation value and its covariance of a local track in the form [5]

$$\begin{cases} \hat{X}_{ml} = P_{ml}(P_l^{-1}\hat{X}_l + P_r^{-1}\hat{X}_r), \\ P_{ml} = (P_l^{-1} + P_r^{-1})^{-1}. \end{cases} \tag{6.26}$$

Through the above process, we can yield the Regions of Interest (ROIs) using global tracks. Moreover, we can extract more accurate environment structure using visual information. In our approach, the CCD sensors implement lane recognition and vehicle detection. Our lane recognition approach is an Adaptive Randomized Hough Transform (ARHT) [12] described in Sect. 4.3, which implements robust and accurate detection of lane markings without manual initialization or priori information under road environment. The results of lane recognition provide the road structure and limit the region of obstacles. In terms of vehicle detection, we use Gabor features to represent and detect vehicles in ROIs [4]. Figure 6.6 shows the fusion results of the three sensors at the Springrobot platform shown in Fig. 6.5.

## 6.5 Conclusion and Future Work

In our approach, we have proposed an interactive road situation analysis framework and its algorithmic implementation, namely the multiple-sensor multi-object

Fig. 6.5 Intelligent driver assistance and safety warning platform—Springrobot

Fig. 6.6 Obstacles tracks using our approach

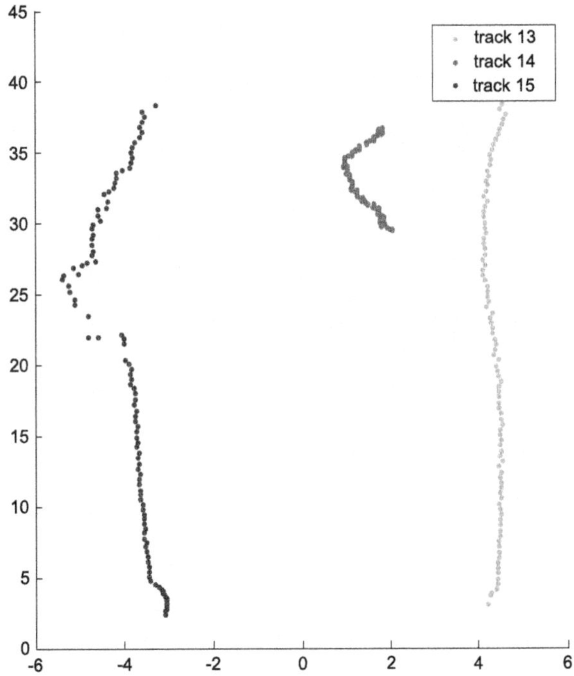

detection and tracking approach. We put emphasis on the future situation evaluation rather than current obstacles situation. Vehicle dynamics and driver behavior are considered as two influencing factors for various $I^2$DASW systems. In addition, comparing other similar systems, our framework is a more integrated one, where the control module based on preview-following is involved, which yields a concise and efficient framework.

There are also several questions that need to be further investigated in our future work. For special applications, deciding how to select and setup the sensor network is also very important. We calibrate the sensors in our system, and it is normally the case that it needs many manual operations. Needless to say, joint calibration of a multiple-sensor including a camera, lidar and a radar is desired to be automatically made in all driver assistance and safety warning systems.

## References

1. Alefs, B., Schreiber, D., Clabian, M.: Hypothesis based vehicle detection for increased simplicity in multi-sensor ACC. In: Proc. of the IEEE Intelligent Vehicles Symposium, pp. 261–266 (2005)
2. Baehring, D., Simon, S., Niehsen, W., Stiller, C.: Detection of close cut-in and overtaking vehicles for driver assistance based on planar parallax. In: Proc. of the IEEE Intelligent Vehicles Symposium (2005)
3. Bar-Shalom, Y., Li, X., Kirubarajan, T., Wiley, J.: Estimation with Applications to Tracking and Navigation. Wiley, New York (2001)
4. Cheng, H., Zheng, N., Sun, C., van de Wetering, H.: Vanishing point and Gabor feature based multi-resolution on-road vehicle detection. In: International Symposium on Neural Networks, pp. 46–51 (2006)
5. Escamilla-Ambrosio, P., Lieven, N.: A multiple-sensor multiple-target tracking approach for the autotaxi system. In: Proc. of the IEEE Intelligent Vehicles Symposium, pp. 601–606 (2004)
6. Fang, Y., Masaki, I., Horn, B.: Depth-Based Target Segmentation for Intelligent Vehicles: Fusion of Radar and Binocular Stereo (2002)
7. Gern, A., Franke, U., Levi, P.: Advanced lane recognition-fusing vision and radar. In: Proc. of the IEEE Intelligent Vehicles Symposium (2000)
8. Hofmann, U., Rieder, A., Dickmanns, E.: EMS-vision: application to hybrid adaptive cruise control. In: Proc. of the IEEE Intelligent Vehicles Symposium (2000)
9. Kaempchen, N., Buehler, M., Dietmayer, K.: Feature-level fusion for free-form object tracking using laserscanner and video. In: Proc. of the IEEE Intelligent Vehicles Symposium, pp. 453–458 (2005)
10. Kawasaki, N., Kiencke, U.: Standard platform for sensor fusion on advanced driver assistance system using Bayesian network. In: Proc. of the IEEE Intelligent Vehicles Symposium, pp. 250–255 (2004)
11. Kolodko, J., Vlacic, L.: Fusion of range and vision for real-time motion estimation. In: Proc. of the IEEE Intelligent Vehicles Symposium, pp. 256–261 (2004)
12. Li, Q., Zheng, N., Cheng, H.: Springrobot: A prototype autonomous vehicle and its algorithms for lane detection. IEEE Trans. Intell. Transp. Syst. **5**(4), 300–308 (2004)
13. Mendes, A., Bento, L., Nunes, U.: Multi-target detection and tracking with a laser scanner. In: IEEE International Intelligent Vehicle Symposium, pp. 796–801 (2004)
14. Mobus, R., Kolbe, U.: Multi-target multi-object tracking, sensor fusion of radar and infrared. In: Proc. of the IEEE Intelligent Vehicles Symposium, pp. 732–737 (2004)

15. Qin, J.: Study on obstacle detection and tracking based on multi-sensor fusion. Relax Master Thesis, Xi'an Jiaotong University, Xi'an, China (2005)
16. Ruder, M., Enkelmann, W., Garnitz, R.: Highway lane change assistant. In: IEEE Intelligent Vehicle Symposium (2002)
17. Shimomura, N., Fujimoto, K., Oki, T., Muro, H.: An algorithm for distinguishing the types of objects on the road using laser radar and vision. IEEE Trans. Intell. Transp. Syst. **3**(3), 189–195 (2002)
18. Srinivasa, N., Chen, Y., Daniell, C.: A fusion system for real-time forward collision warning in automobiles. Proc. IEEE Intell. Trans. Syst. Conf. **1**, 457–462 (2003)

# Part III
# Vehicle Localization and Navigation

# Chapter 7
# An Integrated DGPS/IMU Positioning Approach

## 7.1 Introduction

For autonomous navigation, vehicles must be capable of determining their global and local positions within their surrounding environment [10, 19, 27]. However, vehicle localization is one of challenging problems due to the following issues. First of all, sensor noises give rise to inaccurate position information in global localization. If the vehicle can obtain the accurate global position information, we would simplify localization problem a lot. Unfortunately, the precision of the nowadays GPS is about several meters. Though differential GPS can provide the promising resolution of several centimeters, on-vehicle GPS terminals could hardly receive any signals especially in some urban environments. In addition, other sensors' noises (cameras, sonar, etc.) also degrade the localization a lot. Second, vehicle location localization is not only to obtain the absolute position, but also to capture relative position relationship between a host vehicle and its surrounding objects. This plays an important role in obstacle avoidance.

The commonly-used positioning sensors are the Global Navigation Satellite System (GNSS), Inertial Measurement Unit (IMU), and encoders. The basic elements of the GNSS are the set of satellites, ground augmentation systems, and user equipment. There are four GNSS over the world: Global Positioning System (GPS) [15, 16], GLONASS [17], Galileo [3], and BeiDou/Compass [4, 14]. Among these GNSS, GPS is the most commonly-used for vehicle navigation and localization. As we mentioned before, the GNSS cannot provide accurate positioning information at any time or any place. Hence, combining IMU and encoders is capable of compensating for the disadvantages of the GNSS. The GNSS and DR are usually mutually complementary. On the one hand, the GNSS provides the absolute position to an IMU for both the initialization of the vehicle position and for sensor correction. On the other hand, the result of an IMU could compensate the random errors of the GNSS. As a result, combining two approaches can overcome the disadvantages of each single approach, thus improving positioning precision [1, 23].

Many problems in vehicle localization and navigation require estimating the states of a system that change over time using noisy time sequences. The state–space representation to dynamic time sequence modeling provides the state vectors

H. Cheng, *Autonomous Intelligent Vehicles*,
Advances in Computer Vision and Pattern Recognition,
DOI 10.1007/978-1-4471-2280-7_7, © Springer-Verlag London Limited 2011

of a system and the relationship between state vectors and measurements. Moreover, to inference a dynamic system, both a system model and a measurement model are necessary in a deterministic/probabilistic form. In terms of linear/Gaussian systems, Kalman filtering approaches are linear least square-root estimators [12]. Though Kalman filtering was originally developed for a linear system, the Extended Kalman Filtering is used to handle nonlinear cases by approximating nonlinear functions using partial derivatives [18]. However, all of the previous approaches fail for multimodal pdfs and heavily skewed distributions.

In this case, the system models could be both nonlinear and non-Gaussian. Hence, particle filtering, a.k.a. Sequential Monte Carlo filtering, is applied to represent the state distribution using particles [11, 13]. In recent years, this approach is widely used in robot localization [11, 13, 22] and sensor fusion [25].

## 7.2 Related Work

The GPS has been widely used in vehicle navigation [5, 7, 24]. However, this kind of positioning systems based solely on GPS does not work well when the GPS signals are very bad due to either object blocking or not enough satellites. Therefore, many real-world positioning systems integrate the GPS with dead reckoning sensors to provide better positioning solutions. Moreover, KF/EKF/UKF/PF based techniques are widely used to both fuse the GPS data and DR data, and iteratively estimate vehicle position [2, 28].

In the last 30 years, integrated GPS/DR approaches are widely used in vehicle navigation [1, 27]. Abbott et al. presented a quantitative examination of the impact that individual navigation sensors have on the performance of a vehicle navigation system [1]. Gamini et al. investigated building an environment map while simultaneously calculating the absolute position using this map in an unknown environment [8]. Cui et al. proposed a vehicle positioning approach with GPS especially in urban canyon environments where the GPS signals are easy to be blocked by high buildings, thus yielding insufficient satellite coverage. To this end, the authors presented a constrained method by approximating vehicle path using line segments. By doing so, the system can reduce the minimum number of required available satellites to two. In recent years, Vehicle AdHoc Networks (VANets) are playing an important role in communicating to provide various applications varying from safe driving to assisted driving. Boukerche et al. discussed the positioning requirements of the main VANet applications based on data fusion techniques [5]. Moreover, the authors investigated how to combine these positioning techniques using data fusion to obtain robust positioning solutions in VANets. In TELEcommunications and inforMATICS (TELEMATICS) systems, a car navigation system plays a core role in both safe and comfortable driving. Low-cost DR systems are critical for extending a commercial navigation market. To this end, Cho et al. presented a low-cost GPS/DR system where the DR system consists of an accelerometer and a gyro [6]. Moreover, the authors investigated the performance of three estimating techniques, EKF, Sigma-Point KF (SPKF), and the Sigma-Point-based Receding-HKF (SPRHKF), in various

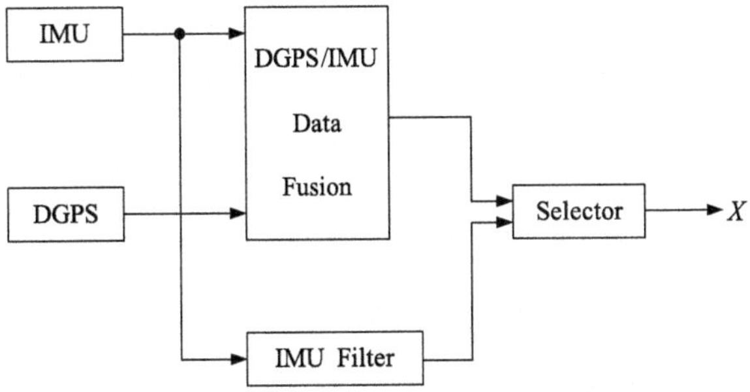


**Fig. 7.1** The framework of the DGPS/IMU positioning system

situations. Yang et al. proposed a nonlinear filter algorithm for GPS/DR positioning system, combining SR-KF and SR-UKF [24]. The experimental results show that the proposed algorithm has both higher filtering precision and better stability than those of the EKF. As we know, in-car positioning and navigation systems not only guide drivers from one location to another by GPS/DR and a map, but also provide communication service. Skog et al. presented data sources and fusion techniques for an in-car navigation system [20]. Also, the authors introduced the advantages and disadvantages of the four commonly used basic positioning sensors.

## 7.3 An Integrated DGPS/IMU Positioning Approach

In a GPS/IMU navigation system, IMU provides position, velocity, and pose, while GPS provides position information for correcting IMU in general [9, 26]. However, in our navigation system, we directly use the observed data from the DGPS as input of GPS/IMU data fusion, without requiring separate DGPS filters. When DGPS does not work well, IMU will provide localizing parameters, shown in Fig. 7.1. The robust DGPS/IMU data fusion and IMU Filter are described below.

### *7.3.1 The System Equation*

In this section, we assume that land vehicles are moving objects in 2D planes. Let $X^T = [e\ n\ \dot{e}\ \dot{n}\ \ddot{e}\ \ddot{n}\ \epsilon_e\ \epsilon_n\ \delta_\theta\ \delta_s]$ denote a state vector, where $e$ and $n$ are the coordinates in the $x$- and $y$-directions, respectively; $\dot{e}/\dot{n}$ and $\ddot{e}/\ddot{n}$ are the velocity and acceleration in the $x$- or $y$-directions; $\epsilon_e$ and $\epsilon_n$ are the position errors in the $x$- and $y$-directions, respectively; $\delta_\theta$ and $\delta_s$ are the relative rotating angle error of gyros and the distance error of encoders.

As we know, we have the following equation from Newton's laws of motion

$$\begin{cases} s = vt + \frac{1}{2}at^2, \\ v = at, \end{cases} \tag{7.1}$$

where $t$ is the time, $v$ is the velocity, $a$ is the acceleration, and $s$ is the distance. From (7.1), we can see that both the distance and velocity are calculated from acceleration. Though driving tasks are quite complex due to the effects of routines, road surfaces, drivers, and traffic jams. The state change of a vehicle is provided either directly or indirectly from the acceleration change. Therefore, it is important to model acceleration change for building dynamic models of the vehicle.

There are many operations in vehicle driving, such as making a turn, accelerating, decelerating and stopping a car, due to the complexity of urban traffic environment. Hence, the acceleration of a vehicle is represented using the "current" model [21, 28, 29], and then the acceleration change of the vehicle is a first-order stationary Markov process

$$\ddot{e} = \bar{a}_e + a_e, \qquad \dot{a}_e = -\tau_{a_e} \cdot a_e + W_{a_e}, \tag{7.2}$$

$$\ddot{n} = \bar{a}_n + a_n, \qquad \dot{a}_n = -\tau_{a_n} \cdot a_n + W_{a_n}, \tag{7.3}$$

where $a_e$ and $a_n$ are zero-mean Singer acceleration processes; $\bar{a}_e$ and $\bar{a}_n$ are the means of acceleration in the $x$- and $y$-directions, respectively; $W_{a_e}$ and $W_{a_n}$ are zero-mean white noises with constant power spectral densities $2\tau_{a_e}\sigma_{a_e}^2$ and $2\tau_{a_n}\sigma_{a_n}^2$, respectively; $\tau_{a_e}$ and $\tau_{a_n}$ are the multiplicative inverses of correlation time constants. At the same time, we model the other errors as a first-order Markov process as follows

$$\begin{cases} \dot{\epsilon}_e = -\tau_{\epsilon_e}\epsilon_e + \omega_{\epsilon_e}, & \dot{\epsilon}_n = -\tau_{\epsilon_n}\epsilon_n + \omega_{\epsilon_n}, \\ \dot{\delta}_\theta = -\tau_{\delta_\theta}\delta_\theta + \omega_{\delta_\theta}, & \delta_s = -\tau_{\delta_s}\delta_s + \omega_{\delta_s}, \end{cases} \tag{7.4}$$

where $\tau_{\epsilon_e}$, $\tau_{\epsilon_n}$, $\tau_{\delta_\theta}$, $\tau_{\delta_s}$ are the multiplicative inverses of correlation time constants; $W_{\epsilon_e}$, $W_{\epsilon_n}$, $W_{\delta_\theta}$, $W_{\delta_s}$ are zero-mean white noises. Hence, we obtain the discrete state equation described as

$$X_{k+1} = \Phi_{k+1,k} X_k + U_k + W_k, \tag{7.5}$$

where

$$\Phi_{k+1,k} = \begin{bmatrix} I_{2\times2} & T I_{2\times2} & C_1 & \mathbf{0}_{2\times2} & \mathbf{0}_{2\times2} \\ \mathbf{0}_{2\times2} & I_{2\times2} & C_2 & \mathbf{0}_{2\times2} & \mathbf{0}_{2\times2} \\ \mathbf{0}_{2\times2} & \mathbf{0}_{2\times2} & E_1 & \mathbf{0}_{2\times2} & \mathbf{0}_{2\times2} \\ \mathbf{0}_{2\times2} & \mathbf{0}_{2\times2} & \mathbf{0}_{2\times2} & E_2 & \mathbf{0}_{2\times2} \\ \mathbf{0}_{2\times2} & \mathbf{0}_{2\times2} & \mathbf{0}_{2\times2} & \mathbf{0}_{2\times2} & 20F \end{bmatrix},$$

$$C_1 = \mathrm{diag}\left\{ \frac{1}{\tau_{a_e}^2}\left(-1 + \tau_{a_e}T + e^{-\tau_{a_e}T}\right), \frac{1}{\tau_{a_n}^2}\left(-1 + \tau_{a_n}T + e^{-\tau_{a_n}T}\right) \right\},$$

$$C_2 = \mathrm{diag}\left\{ \frac{1}{\tau_{a_e}}\left(1 - e^{-\tau_{a_e}T}\right), \frac{1}{\tau_{a_n}}\left(1 - e^{-\tau_{a_n}T}\right) \right\},$$

$$E_1 = \mathrm{diag}\left\{ e^{-\tau_{a_e}T}, e^{-\tau_{a_n}T} \right\}, \qquad E_2 = \mathrm{diag}\left\{ e^{-\tau_{\varepsilon_e}T}, e^{-\tau_{\varepsilon_n}T} \right\},$$

$$F = \mathrm{diag}\left\{ e^{-\tau_{\delta_\theta}T}, e^{-\tau_{\delta_s}T} \right\},$$

$$U_k = [u_1,\ u_2,\ u_3,\ u_4,\ u_5,\ u_6,\ I_{1\times 4}]^T,$$

$$u_1 = \frac{1}{\tau_{a_e}}\left(-T + \frac{\tau_{a_e} T^2}{2} + \frac{1-e^{-\tau_{a_e} T}}{\tau_{a_e}}\right)\bar{a}_e,$$

$$u_2 = \frac{1}{\tau_{a_n}}\left(-T + \frac{\tau_{a_n} T^2}{2} + \frac{1-e^{-\tau_{a_n} T}}{\tau_{a_n}}\right)\bar{a}_n,$$

$$u_3 = \left(T - \frac{1-e^{-\tau_{a_e} T}}{\tau_{a_e}}\right)\bar{a}_e, \qquad u_4 = \left(T - \frac{1-e^{-\tau_{a_n} T}}{\tau_{a_n}}\right)\bar{a}_n\ ,$$

$$u_5 = \left(1 - e^{-\tau_{a_e}} T\right)\bar{a}_e, \qquad u_6 = \left(1 - e^{-\tau_{a_n}} T\right)\bar{a}_n.$$

$W_k$ is a white noise sequence, $E[W_k W_{k+j}^T] = 0$ $(\forall j \neq 0)$, and its covariance matrix is

$$Q_k = E\left[W_k W_k^T\right] = \begin{bmatrix} Q_{11} & \mathbf{0}_{6\times 2} & \mathbf{0}_{6\times 2} \\ \mathbf{0}_{2\times 6} & Q_{12} & \mathbf{0}_{2\times 2} \\ \mathbf{0}_{2\times 6} & \mathbf{0}_{2\times 2} & 20Q_{13} \end{bmatrix}, \tag{7.6}$$

where

$$Q_{11} = [q_{ij}]_{6\times 6},$$

$$q_{11} = \frac{\sigma_{a_e}^2}{\tau_{a_e}^4}\left[1 - e^{-2\tau_{a_e} T} + 2\tau_{a_e} T + \frac{2\tau_{a_e}^3 T^3}{3} - 2\tau_{a_e}^2 T^2 - 4\tau_{a_e} T e^{-\tau_{a_e} T}\right],$$

$$q_{13} = q_{31} = \frac{\sigma_{a_e}^2}{\tau_{a_e}^3}\left[e^{-2\tau_{a_e} T} + 1 - 2e^{-\tau_{a_e} T} + 2\tau_{a_e} T e^{-\tau_{a_e} T} - 2\tau_{a_e} T + \tau_{a_e}^2 T^2\right],$$

$$q_{15} = q_{51} = \frac{\sigma_{a_e}^2}{\tau_{a_e}^2}\left[1 - e^{-2\tau_{a_e} T} - 2\tau_{a_e} T e^{-\tau_{a_e} T}\right],$$

$$q_{22} = \frac{\sigma_{a_n}^2}{\tau_{a_n}^4}\left[1 - e^{-2\tau_{a_n} T} + 2\tau_{a_n} T + \frac{2\tau_{a_n}^3 T^3}{3} - 2\tau_{a_n}^2 T^2 - 4\tau_{a_n} T e^{-\tau_{a_n} T}\right],$$

$$q_{24} = q_{42} = \frac{\sigma_{a_n}^2}{\tau_{a_n}^3}\left[e^{-2\tau_{a_n} T} + 1 - 2e^{-\tau_{a_n} T} + 2\tau_{a_n} T e^{-\tau_{a_n} T} - 2\tau_{a_n} T + \tau_{a_n}^2 T^2\right],$$

$$q_{26} = q_{62} = \frac{\sigma_{a_n}^2}{\tau_{a_n}^2}\left[1 - e^{-2\tau_{a_n} T} - 2\tau_{a_n} T e^{-\tau_{a_n} T}\right],$$

$$q_{33} = \frac{\sigma_{a_e}^2}{\tau_{a_e}^2}\left[4e^{-\tau_{a_e} T} - 3 - e^{-2\tau_{a_e} T} + 2\tau_{a_e} T\right],$$

$$q_{35} = q_{53} = \frac{\sigma_{a_e}^2}{\tau_{a_e}}\left[e^{-2\tau_{a_e} T} + 1 - 2e^{-\tau_{a_e} T}\right],$$

$$q_{44} = \frac{\sigma_{a_n}^2}{\tau_{a_e}^2}\left[4e^{-\tau_{a_n}T} - 3 - e^{-2\tau_{a_n}T} + 2\tau_{a_n}T\right],$$

$$q_{46} = q_{64} = \frac{\sigma_{a_n}^2}{\tau_{a_n}}\left[e^{-2\tau_{a_n}T} + 1 - 2e^{-\tau_{a_n}T}\right],$$

$$q_{55} = \sigma_{a_e}^2\left[1 - e^{-2\tau_{a_e}T}\right],$$

$$q_{66} = \sigma_{a_n}^2\left[1 - e^{-2\tau_{a_n}T}\right], \quad \text{the other } q_{ij} = 0,$$

$$Q_{12} = \mathrm{diag}\left\{\sigma_{\varepsilon_e}^2\left(1 - e^{-2\tau_{\varepsilon_e}T}\right),\ \sigma_{\varepsilon_n}^2\left(1 - e^{-2\tau_{\varepsilon_n}T}\right)\right\},$$

$$Q_{13} = \mathrm{diag}\left\{\sigma_{\delta_\theta}^2\left(1 - e^{-2\tau_{\delta_\theta}T}\right), \sigma_{\delta_s}^2\left(1 - e^{-2\tau_{\delta_s}T}\right)\right\}.$$

### 7.3.2 The Measurement Equation

In this section, we can obtain position and velocity, $e_r$, $n_r$, $\dot{e}_r$ and $\dot{e}_n$, from DGPS devices, the distance $S$ from odometers, and the rotation angle $Q$ from gyroscopes. Furthermore, the relationships between the state vectors and the measurement vectors are described as

$$Z_k = [z_{k,1}, z_{k,2}, \ldots, z_{k,6}]^T, \tag{7.7}$$

where

$$z_{k,1} = e_r(k) = e(k) + \varepsilon_e(k) + v_1(k),$$

$$z_{k,2} = n_r(k) = n(k) + \varepsilon_n(k) + v_2(k),$$

$$z_{k,3} = \dot{e}_r(k) = \dot{e}(k) + v_3(k),$$

$$z_{k,4} = \dot{n}_r(k) = \dot{n}(k) + v_4(k),$$

$$z_{k,5} = Q(k) = \alpha(k) - \beta(k-1) + \delta_\theta(k) + v_5(k), \quad \alpha(k) = \arctan\frac{\dot{e}(k)}{\dot{n}(k)} + \gamma,$$

$$(\gamma = 0, -\pi \text{ or } \pi), \quad \beta(k-1) = \alpha(0) + \sum_{i=1}^{k-1}\left[Q(i) + \delta_\theta(i)\right],$$

$$z_{k,6} = S(k) = T\sqrt{\dot{e}^2(k) + \dot{n}^2(k)} + \delta_s(k) + v_6(k).$$

Note that $v_i(k)$ $(k = 1, 2, \ldots, 6)$ is a zero-mean Gaussian white noise sequence with the covariance matrix $R(k) = \mathrm{diag}\{r_1^2, r_2^2, \ldots, r_6^2\}$ and $V_k = [v_1(k), v_2(k), \ldots, v_6(k)]^T$.

Hence, we obtain the measurement equation

$$Z_k = h[X_k] + V_k = H_{1,k}X_k + H_{2,k}[X_k] + V_k, \tag{7.8}$$

where

$$H_{1,k} = \begin{bmatrix} 1 & 0 & 0 & 0 & 0 & 0 & 1 & 0 & 0 & 0 \\ 0 & 1 & 0 & 0 & 0 & 0 & 0 & 1 & 0 & 0 \\ 0 & 0 & 1 & 0 & 0 & 0 & 0 & 0 & 0 & 0 \\ 0 & 0 & 0 & 1 & 0 & 0 & 0 & 0 & 0 & 0 \end{bmatrix},$$

$$H_{2,k}[X_k] = \begin{bmatrix} \alpha(k) - \beta(k-1) + \delta_\theta(k) \\ T\sqrt{\dot{e}^2(k) + \dot{n}^2(k)} + \delta_s(k) \end{bmatrix}.$$

Since (7.8) is a nonlinear equation, there are many potential choices to linearize it, thus yielding the solution [24]. Here, we use Extended Kalman filtering (EKF) by linearly approximating nonlinear measurement system around the last state estimate

$$\dot{Z}_k \approx h[X_{k,k-1}] + H[X_{k,k-1}][X_k - X_{k,k-1}] + V_k, \tag{7.9}$$

where

$$H[X_{k,k-1}] = \begin{bmatrix} I_{2\times2} & \mathbf{0}_{2\times2} & \mathbf{0}_{2\times2} & I_{2\times2} & \mathbf{0}_{2\times2} \\ \mathbf{0}_{2\times2} & I_{2\times2} & \mathbf{0}_{2\times2} & \mathbf{0}_{2\times2} & \mathbf{0}_{2\times2} \\ \mathbf{0}_{2\times2} & H_{2\times2} & \mathbf{0}_{2\times2} & \mathbf{0}_{2\times2} & I_{2\times2} \end{bmatrix},$$

$$H_{2\times2} = \begin{bmatrix} \frac{\dot{n}}{\dot{e}^2+\dot{n}^2} & -\frac{\dot{e}}{\dot{e}^2+\dot{n}^2} \\ \frac{T\dot{e}}{\sqrt{\dot{e}^2+\dot{n}^2}} & \frac{T\dot{n}}{\sqrt{\dot{e}^2+\dot{n}^2}} \end{bmatrix}\Bigg|_{X_{k,k-1}}.$$

Letting $\Phi[X_{k,k-1}] = Z_k - h[X_{k,k-1}] + H[X_{k,k-1}]X_{k,k-1}$, we have

$$\Phi[X_{k,k-1}] \approx H[X_{k,k-1}]X_k + V_k, \tag{7.10}$$

Equation (7.10) is a linearized measurement equation. Note that a fundamental advantage of the EKF is that the distributions of the random variables are no longer Gaussian, and the EKF only approximates the optimality of the Bayes' rule by linearization.

### 7.3.3 Data Fusion Using EKF

Upon both (7.5) and (7.10), we use a nonzero mean-adaptive acceleration model to represent acceleration change [28]. Therefore, we can obtain an adaptive Kalman filtering algorithm stated below:

1.

$$X_{k,k-1} = \Phi'_{k,k-1}X_{k-1},$$

where

$$\Phi'_{k,k-1} = \begin{bmatrix} I_{2\times 2} & TI_{2\times 2} & \frac{T^2}{2} I_{2\times 2} & \mathbf{0}_{2\times 2} & \mathbf{0}_{2\times 2} \\ \mathbf{0}_{2\times 2} & I_{2\times 2} & TI_{2\times 2} & \mathbf{0}_{2\times 2} & \mathbf{0}_{2\times 2} \\ \mathbf{0}_{2\times 2} & \mathbf{0}_{2\times 2} & I_{2\times 2} & \mathbf{0}_{2\times 2} & \mathbf{0}_{2\times 2} \\ \mathbf{0}_{2\times 2} & \mathbf{0}_{2\times 2} & \mathbf{0}_{2\times 2} & E_2 & \mathbf{0}_{2\times 2} \\ \mathbf{0}_{2\times 2} & \mathbf{0}_{2\times 2} & \mathbf{0}_{2\times 2} & \mathbf{0}_{2\times 2} & \Phi_2 \end{bmatrix}.$$

We would like to point out that $\Phi'_{k,k-1}$ is used to replace $\Phi_{k,k-1}$. The rationale behind this is that it is equivalent to increase the sampling rate ($T \to 0$). For the details, we refer to [28].

2.

$$P_{k,k-1} = \Phi_{k,k-1} P_{k-1} \Phi^T_{k,k-1} + Q_{k-1},$$

$$P'_{k,k-1} = \widetilde{\Phi}_{k,k-1} P'_{k-1} \widetilde{\Phi}^T_{k,k-1} + \widetilde{Q}_{k-1},$$

where

$$\widetilde{\Phi}_{k,k-1} = \begin{bmatrix} I_{2\times 2} & TI_{2\times 2} & C_1 & \mathbf{0}_{2\times 2} \\ \mathbf{0}_{2\times 2} & I_{2\times 2} & C_2 & \mathbf{0}_{2\times 2} \\ \mathbf{0}_{2\times 2} & \mathbf{0}_{2\times 2} & E_1 & \mathbf{0}_{2\times 2} \\ \mathbf{0}_{2\times 2} & \mathbf{0}_{2\times 2} & \mathbf{0}_{2\times 2} & E_2 \end{bmatrix}, \qquad \widetilde{Q}_{k-1} = \begin{bmatrix} Q_{11} & \mathbf{0}_{6\times 2} \\ \mathbf{0}_{2\times 6} & Q_{12} \end{bmatrix}.$$

3.

$$K_k = P_{k,k-1} H^T[X_{k,k-1}] \big\{ H[X_{k,k-1}] P_{k,k-1} H^T[X_{k,k-1}] + R_k \big\}^{-1},$$

$$K'_k = P'_{k,k-1} H'^T[X_{k,k-1}] \big\{ H'[X_{k,k-1}] P'_{k,k-1} H'^T[X_{k,k-1}] + R'_k \big\}^{-1}.$$

4.

$$X_k = X_{k,k-1} + \big[ G_1^T \; G_2^T \big]^T,$$

where $G_1 = K'_k\{Z'_k - h_1[X_{k,k-1}]\}$, $G_2 = [g_1, g_2]^T$, and $g_1$ and $g_2$ are ninth and tenth elements of the vector $K_k\{Z_k - h[X_{k,k-1}]\}$.

5.

$$P'_k = \big[ I - K'_k H'_k \big] P'_{k,k-1}, \qquad P_k = \big\{ I - K_k H[X_{k,k-1}] \big\} P_{k,k-1}.$$

When a vehicle cannot get DGPS signals at time $k'$, the above equation cannot be used to get a correct solution. In this case, the data fusion stops. Therefore, the following equations provide vehicle position

$$e_{k'} = e_{k'-1} + s_{k'} \sin[\beta_{k'-1} + \theta_{k'}], \qquad n_{k'} = n_{k'-1} + s_{k'} \cos[\beta_{k'-1} + \theta_{k'}].$$

## References

1. Abbott, E., Powell, D.: Land-vehicle navigation using GPS. Proc. IEEE **87**(1), 145–162 (1999)

2. Bar-Shalom, Y., Li, X., Kirubarajan, T., Wiley, J.: Estimation with Applications to Tracking and Navigation. Wiley, New York (2001)
3. Benedicto, J., Dinwiddy, S., Gatti, G., Lucas, R., Lugert, M.: GALILEO: Satellite System Design. European Space Agency (2000)
4. Bian, S., Jin, J., Fang, Z.: The Beidou satellite positioning system and its positioning accuracy. Navigation **52**(3), 123–129 (2005)
5. Boukerche, A., Oliveira, H., Nakamura, E., Loureiro, A.: Vehicular ad hoc networks: A new challenge for localization-based systems. Comput. Commun. **31**(12), 2838–2849 (2008)
6. Cho, S., Choi, W.: Robust positioning technique in low-cost DR/GPS for land navigation. IEEE Trans. Instrum. Meas. **55**(4), 1132–1142 (2006)
7. Cui, Y., Ge, S.: Autonomous vehicle positioning with GPS in urban canyon environments. IEEE Trans. Robot. Autom. **19**(1), 15–25 (2003)
8. Dissanayake, M., Newman, P., Clark, S., Durrant-Whyte, H., Csorba, M.: A solution to the simultaneous localization and map building (SLAM) problem. IEEE Trans. Robot. Autom. **17**(3), 229–241 (2001)
9. Dong, X., Zhang, S., Hua, Z.: Integrated GPS/INS Navigation and Its Application (1998)
10. Durrant-Whyte, H.: Where am I? A tutorial on mobile vehicle localization. Int. J. Indust. Robot **21**(2), 11–16 (1994)
11. Fox, D., Thrun, S., Burgard, W., Dellaert, F.: Particle Filters for Mobile Robot Localization (2001)
12. Grewal, M., Andrews, A., Corporation, E.: Kalman Filtering: Theory and Practice using MATLAB. Wiley, New York (2001)
13. Gustafsson, F., Gunnarsson, F., Bergman, N., Forssell, U., Jansson, J., Karlsson, R., Nordlund, P.: Particle filters for positioning, navigation, and tracking. IEEE Trans. Signal Process. **50**(2), 425–437 (2002)
14. Hegarty, C., Chatre, E.: Evolution of the Global Navigation Satellite System (GNSS). Proc. IEEE **96**(12), 1902–1917 (2008)
15. Hofmann-Wellenhof, B., Lichtenegger, H., Collins, J.: GPS: Theory and Practice. Springer, Berlin (1994)
16. Kaplan, E., Hegarty, C.: Understanding GPS: Principles and Applications. Artech House, Norwood (2006)
17. Langley, R.: Glonass: review and update. GPS World **8**(7), 46–51 (1997)
18. McGee, L.: Discovery of the Kalman Filter as a Practical Tool for Aerospace and Industry (1985)
19. Siegwart, R., Nourbakhsh, I.: Introduction to Autonomous Mobile Robots. MIT Press, Cambridge (2004)
20. Skog, I., Handel, P.: In-car positioning and navigation technologies—a survey. IEEE Trans. Intell. Transp. Syst. **10**(1), 4–21 (2009)
21. Tang, J.: Fuzzy Controller Design and Integrated Navigation for Intelligent Vehicles (2005)
22. Thrun, S.: Probabilistic robotics. Commun. ACM **45**(3), 52–57 (2002)
23. Vicek, C., McLain, P., Murphy, M.: GPS/dead reckoning for vehicle tracking in the urban canyon environment. In: Proc. of the IEEE Vehicle Navigation and Information Systems Conference, vol. A-34, pp. 461 (1993)
24. Yang, J., Zheng, N.: Integrated positioning algorithm for GPS/DR based on SR-UKF. J. Syst. Simul. (2009)
25. Yang, N., Tian, W., Jin, Z., Zhang, C.: Particle filter for sensor fusion in a land vehicle navigation system. Meas. Sci. Technol. **16**, 677 (2005)
26. Yang, X., He, H.: GPS/DR integrated navigation system based on adaptive robust Kalman filtering. IEEE Int. Conf. Microwave Millimeter Wave Technol. **4**, 1946–1949 (2008)
27. Zhao, Y., House, A.: Vehicle location and navigation systems: Intelligent transportation systems. Artech House, Norwood, pp. 221–224 (1997)
28. Zhou, H., Jiang, Z., Peide, W.: Tracking of Maneuvering Targets. Publication of Defense Industry, Beijing (1991)
29. Zhou, H., Kumar, K.: A current statistical model and adaptive algorithm for estimating maneuvering targets. AIAA J. Guidance **7**, 596–602 (1984)

# Chapter 8
# Vehicle Navigation Using Global Views

## 8.1 Introduction

Driver inattention is a major offender to highway crashes. The National Highway Traffic Safety Administration estimates that at least 25% of police-reported crashes involve some forms of driver inattention [15]. Driving is a process that requires a driver to distribute his/her attention among different sub-tasks. First of all, a driver needs to pay attention to issues directly related to safety, including the surrounding traffic, dashboard displays, and other influx of information on the road such as traffic lights and road signs. In addition, the driver may choose to talk to a passenger, listen to the radio, and talk on the cell phone. Therefore, situation awareness plays an important role in driving safety. In this research, we are developing technologies to provide a driver with the information of dynamic surroundings around the vehicle when he/she is driving to enhance his/her situation awareness.

Situation awareness is defined as the perception of the elements in the environment within a volume of time and space, the comprehension of their meaning, and the projection of their status in the near future [7]. Sensing and representing information is a key for situation awareness in driving a vehicle. A lot of research has been directed towards improving in-vehicle information presentation. Green et al. surveyed early studies on human factor tests in navigation displays [13]. They described objectives, principles and guidelines for the design of in-vehicle devices. Dale et al. investigated the problem of generating natural route descriptions for navigational assistance [6]. Lee et al. developed a situationally appropriate map system for drivers [14].

Navigation user interfaces have changed dramatically over the last few years due to the availability of electronic maps and the Global Positioning System (GPS). The displays in the current GPS navigation systems show the location of a vehicle on a graphical map in a way that is similar to looking straight down at a paper map. Recently, several companies, such as Microsoft and Google, have started providing global view maps, such as aerial imagery maps, satellite imagery maps, and bird's

H. Cheng, *Autonomous Intelligent Vehicles*,
Advances in Computer Vision and Pattern Recognition,
DOI 10.1007/978-1-4471-2280-7_8, 

eye view maps. For example, in the bird's eye view mode, Microsoft's Windows Live Local consists of high resolution aerial imagery taken from an angle rather than straight down from four directions. Besides the GPS, a vehicle can also obtain information about the driving environment from other sensors, such as video cameras mounted at various positions, thermal infrared imagers, RADAR, LIDAR, and ultrasonic sensors [9]. Among these sensors, video cameras are attractive from a packaging and cost perspective. Recent advances in computer vision and image processing technologies have made it possible to apply video-based sensors along with the GPS in driving assistance applications.

Here, we propose a novel method to enhance situation awareness by dynamically providing a global view of surrounding for drivers. The surrounding of a vehicle will be captured by an omnidirectional vision system at the top of a vehicle. In order to obtain high quality of surrounding images, we use an omnidirectional vision system consisting of multiple cameras [2, 5], rather than a catadioptric camera used by the most existing systems for intelligent vehicles [1, 11]. The video stream from the camera is processed to detect nearby vehicles and obstacles. Positions of these detected objects will be overlaid on a global view map of the vehicle. We deduce the mapping between an omnidirectional vision system and global view map. This map can be projected onto a Head-Up Display (HUD) on the windshield and provide a dramatically realistic perspective view of the driving environment. By looking at the display, a driver can have a global picture of the situation and likely produce a good driving strategy.

The rest of this chapter is organized as the following: Sect. 8.2 describes the problem and the proposed approach. Section 8.3 discusses the imaging model of our camera system. Section 8.4 presents a panoramic Inverse Perspective Mapping (pIPM). Section 8.5 shows how to implement the pIPM. Section 8.6 introduces the elimination of the wide-angle lens radial error. In Sect. 8.7, we illustrate the proposed method by an example that maps vehicles detected from the video stream captured by am omnidirectional vision system onto the Google Earth map.

## 8.2 The Problem and Proposed Approach

The field of view, which is the part of the observable world that is seen at any given moment, plays an important role in driving safety. While a human has an almost 180-degree forward-facing field of view, his/her binocular vision, which is important for depth perception, only covers 140 degrees of the field of vision. In a driving situation, it is desirable to have a complete 360-degree field of view. In order to expand a driver's field of view, automobile manufacturers have equipped a rear-view mirror and side mirrors on vehicles. More recently, rear-view video cameras have been added to many new model cars to enhance the ability of the rear-view mirror by showing the road directly behind the car. These camera systems are usually mounted to the bumper or lower parts of the car allowing for better rear visibility. However, looking at mirrors can move a driver's attention away from the road.

**Fig. 8.1** Panorama images taken by a camera array sitting on top of a vehicle

Adding sensors and devices in a vehicle can potentially lead to more distractions. Inattention is one of leading causes of car accidents, estimated to account for 25% of all road traffic accidents. Our goal, therefore, is to increase a driver's field of view without adding distraction sources. In this approach, we propose to capture surroundings of a vehicle by an omnidirectional vision system mounted at the top of a vehicle and display the dynamic global view on the windshield using an HUD. In this way, a driver can obtain a global view of the surrounding without shifting his/her attention away from the front view of the vehicle.

Omnidirectional vision system has been previously used in intelligent vehicle applications, such as vehicle tracking, indoor parking lot, and driver monitoring driver, etc. [8, 10, 11, 16, 17]. These applications used different omnidirectional sensors, such as wide Field-Of-View (FOV) dioptric cameras, catadioptric cameras, Pan-Title-Zoom (PTZ) cameras and polydioptric cameras. Both wide FOV dioptric cameras and catadioptric cameras have some limitations. First, their images are heavily distorted, and we have to spend much time on correcting the distortion. Second, they cannot provide high resolution images of surroundings. PTZ cameras are often used in environment surveillance by moving the cameras. Although PTZ cameras can provide high resolution images, mechanical motion of the cameras causes slow system responses. Instead of using these cameras, we will use an omnidirectional vision system consisting of multiple cameras to capture a full view of the surroundings around a vehicle with the high resolution up to $1600 \times 320$ simultaneously [5]. Figure 8.1 shows examples of two panoramic images captured in our experiment. Rectangles in the images are the detected vehicles.

However, the panoramic video stream from the omnidirectional camera cannot be easily understood by a driver, so we map the driving situation onto a global view map. That is, we automatically extract objects (vehicles, pedestrians, etc.) from the video stream and mark their positions on the global view map. We use a hypothesis–validation structure to detect the nearby vehicles surrounding a host vehicle [4]. Without losing generality, in this approach, we have utilized Google Earth which can provide us with high quality and resolution aerial and satellite images including highways, streets, and more. In addition, data import feature from Google Earth makes it possible to sense and represent the dynamic information surrounding a host vehicle and import our custom geographic data into the Google Earth application.

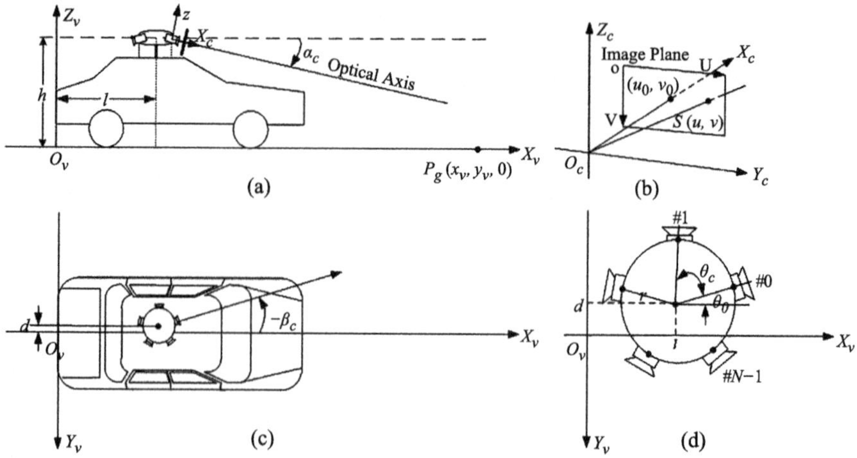


**Fig. 8.2** Geometric relationship among the vehicle, camera array, and image coordinate system of each individual camera: (**a**) front view, (**b**) image plane of an individual camera, (**c**) aerial view, (**d**) camera array layout

## 8.3 The Panoramic Imaging Model

In this section, we describe the mathematical model of panoramic imaging and provide a context for the mapping between the panoramic image and the global electronic map. There are three different coordinate systems as shown in Fig. 8.2. $X_vY_vZ_v$ is the vehicle coordinate system. $X_cY_cZ_c$ is the coordinate system for individual camera $c$ in the camera array where $c = 0, \ldots, N-1$, and $N$ is the number of cameras. $UOV$ is the image coordinate system of camera $c$. Let $r$ denotes the radius of the camera array, and $\theta = 2\pi/N$ the shift angle. The 3D coordinates of the camera array center is $[l, d, h]^T$ in the vehicle coordinate system. The orientation of camera $c$ is defined by two rotation angles $\alpha_c$ and $\beta_c$ as shown in Fig. 8.2(a) and (b).

Assuming the road surface is horizontal, the coordinates of the optical center of camera $c$ in the $X_vY_vZ_v$ coordinate system are

$$T_0^c = [l + r\cos\beta_c, d + r\sin\beta_c, h]^T = \left[l', d', h\right]^T. \tag{8.1}$$

Given any 3D point, let $P_v = [x_v, y_v, z_v]^T$ denote its coordinates in the vehicle coordinate system $X_vY_vZ_v$. Let $P_c = [x_c, y_c, z_c]^T$ denote its coordinates in the camera coordinate system $X_cY_cZ_c$. We have

$$P_v = \begin{bmatrix} \cos\alpha_c\cos\beta_c & \sin\beta_c & -\sin\alpha_c\cos\beta_c \\ -\cos\alpha_c\sin\beta_c & \cos\beta_c & \sin\alpha_c\sin\beta_c \\ \sin\alpha_c & 0 & \cos\alpha_c \end{bmatrix} P_c + T_0^c. \tag{8.2}$$

Consider camera $c$'s image plane $UOV$ as shown in Fig. 8.2(b). Let $(u_0, v_0)$ denote the coordinates of the principal point. According to perspective projection, any point $S(u, v)$ on the image plane satisfies the following equation

$$\frac{y_c}{x_c} = \frac{u - u_0}{f_u}, \qquad \frac{z_c}{x_c} = -\frac{v - v_0}{f_v}, \tag{8.3}$$

where $f_u$, $f_v$ are the scale factors along the $U$- and $V$-axis, respectively.

Let $x_c = t$, $t \in [0, \infty)$, then applying (8.3) yields

$$x_c = t, \qquad y_c = t \cdot \frac{u - u_0}{f_u}, \qquad z_c = -t \cdot \frac{v - v_0}{f_v}. \tag{8.4}$$

Therefore, the parametric equation of line $O_c S$ can be written as

$$[x_c, y_c, z_c]^T = t \cdot \left[1, \frac{u - u_0}{f_u}, -\frac{v - v_0}{f_v}\right]^T. \tag{8.5}$$

Substituting (8.5) into (8.2), we obtain the line equation in the vehicle coordinate system

$$\begin{bmatrix} x_v \\ y_v \\ z_v \end{bmatrix} = t \cdot \mathbf{R} \cdot \begin{bmatrix} 1 \\ \frac{u-u_0}{f_u} \\ -\frac{v-v_0}{f_v} \end{bmatrix} + \begin{bmatrix} l' \\ d' \\ h \end{bmatrix}, \tag{8.6}$$

where $\mathbf{R}$ is the rotation matrix in (8.2).

If we assume the road is flat, the equation of the road plane is $z_v = 0$. Therefore, the intersection of the line $O_c S$ with the road plane can be obtained by setting $z_v = 0$ in (8.6), which yields

$$\begin{cases} x_v(u, v) = h'[u' \ v' \ 1] \begin{bmatrix} \sin\beta_c \\ \sin\alpha_c \cos\beta_c \\ \cos\alpha_c \cos\beta_c \end{bmatrix} + l', \\ y_v(u, v) = h'[u' \ v' \ 1] \begin{bmatrix} \cos\beta_c \\ -\sin\alpha_c \sin\beta_c \\ -\cos\alpha_c \sin\beta_c \end{bmatrix} + d', \end{cases} \tag{8.7}$$

where $h' = \frac{h}{v' \cos\alpha_c - \sin\alpha_c}$, $u' = \frac{u-u_0}{f_u}$, $v' = \frac{v-v_0}{f_v}$.

Note that the object detection is performed on the stitched panoramic image. Given a pixel on the panoramic image, its corresponding positions on the individual camera image planes are obtained from the stitching table, which is generated by a stitching calibration process [5].

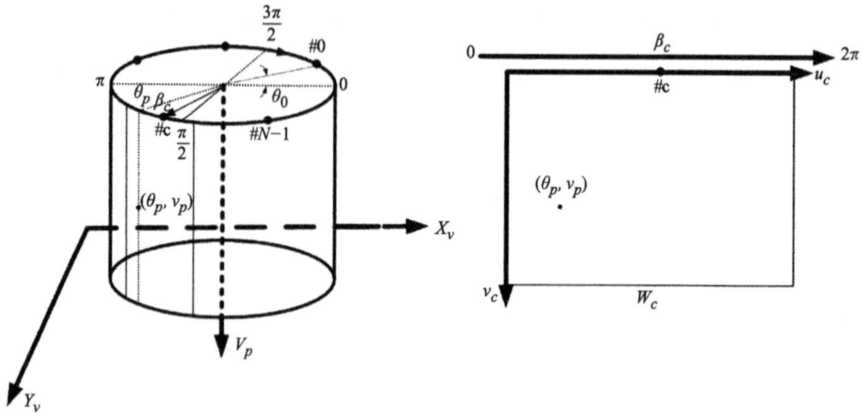


**Fig. 8.3** Mapping from a single image to panoramic image

## 8.4 The Panoramic Inverse Perspective Mapping (pIPM)

### *8.4.1 The Mapping Relationship Between Each Image and a Panoramic Image*

In this section, we build the mapping relationship between each image of its corresponding camera and a panoramic image. Let $(u_c, v_c)$ represent the image coordinates of the $c$th camera. Define the cylindrical panoramic image coordinates captured by all $N$ cameras as $(\theta_p, v_p)$, where $\theta_p \in (0, 2\pi)$ is the panning angle shown in Fig. 8.3. Therefore, we obtain the mapping relationship of the $c$th camera coordinates $(u_c, v_c)$ and panoramic image pixel coordinates $(\theta_p, v_p)$ according to Fig. 8.3 as

$$\begin{cases} \theta_p = \beta_c - \frac{2\pi}{W_p}(u_c + u_0 - W_c), \\ v_p = v_c, \end{cases} \tag{8.8}$$

where $W_c$ is the single image width (here we assume that each camera has same width), $W_p$ is the panoramic image width. To guarantee $\theta_p \in [0, 2\pi)$, we implement the following operation

$$\{\theta_p\}[\bmod 2\pi] = \theta_1, \quad \theta_1 \in [0, 2\pi). \tag{8.9}$$

To simplify the description, we assume that each pixel within a panoramic image is solely from a camera.

### 8.4.2 The Panoramic Inverse Perspective Mapping

From (8.8), we obtain

$$u_c = \frac{W_p}{2\pi}(\theta_p - \beta_c) + (W_c - u_0), \qquad v_c = v_p. \tag{8.10}$$

Substituting (8.10) into (8.6), we obtain the mapping relationship between a pixel $(\theta_p, v_p)$ within the panoramic image and a 3D point $(x_v, y_v, z_v)$ in the vehicle coordinate system as below

$$\begin{bmatrix} x_v \\ y_v \\ z_v \end{bmatrix} = tR\left\{\begin{bmatrix} 1 & 0 & 0 \\ 0 & f_u^{-1} & 0 \\ 0 & 0 & -f_v^{-1} \end{bmatrix}\right.$$
$$\left.\times \left(\begin{bmatrix} 1 & 0 & 0 \\ 0 & -\frac{W_p}{2\pi} & 0 \\ 0 & 0 & 1 \end{bmatrix}\begin{bmatrix} 1 \\ \theta_p \\ v_p \end{bmatrix} + \begin{bmatrix} 0 \\ \frac{W_p}{2\pi}\beta_c + W_c - 2u_0 \\ -v_0 \end{bmatrix}\right)\right\} + T_0^c. \tag{8.11}$$

From (8.1), we know that both the rotation matrix $R$ and the translation vector $T_0^c = [l', d', h]^T$ are functions of $\beta_c$, that is, $R = R(\beta_c)$, $l' = l'(\beta_c)$, $d' = d'(\beta_c)$. The camera external parameter $\beta_c$ is a piecewise linear function of $\theta_p$:

$$\begin{cases} \beta_c(\theta_p) = -\{c\theta_c + \theta_0\}, \\ \theta_p \in (-(\theta_0 - \Delta\theta_u + (c + \frac{1}{2})\theta_c),\ -(\theta_0 - \Delta\theta_u + (c - \frac{1}{2})\theta_c)), \end{cases} \tag{8.12}$$

where $\Delta\theta_u = \frac{2\pi}{W_p}(u_0 - \frac{W_c}{2})$ is a constant that the image center deviates from the camera center; $\theta_0$ is the angle of the #0 camera w.r.t. $X_v$. Similar to (8.8), we implement same operation to guarantee $\beta_c, \theta_p \in [0, 2\pi)$.

Similar to (8.7), substituting road surface constraint equation $z_v = 0$ into (8.11), we obtain the mapping relationship between a 3D point $(x_v, y_v, 0)$ on the road in the vehicle coordinate system and a point $(\theta_p, v_p)$ in the panoramic image in the following form

$$\begin{cases} x_v(\theta_p, v_p) = h'_p[\theta'_p, v'_p, 1]\begin{bmatrix} \sin\beta_c(\theta_p) \\ \sin\alpha_c \cos\beta_c(\theta_p) \\ \cos\alpha_c \cos\beta_c(\theta_p) \end{bmatrix} + l', \\ y_v(\theta_p, v_p) = h'_p[\theta'_p, v'_p, 1]\begin{bmatrix} \cos\beta_c(\theta_p) \\ -\sin\alpha_c \sin\beta_c(\theta_p) \\ -\cos\alpha_c \sin\beta_c(\theta_p) \end{bmatrix} + d', \end{cases} \tag{8.13}$$

where $h'_p = \frac{h}{v'_p \cos\alpha_c - \sin\alpha_c}$, $\theta'_p = \frac{\frac{W_p}{2\pi}(\theta_p - \beta_c) + (W_c - 2u_0)}{f_u}$, $v'_p = \frac{v_p - v_0}{f_v}$. Comparing (8.7) and (8.13), we see that both perspective imaging and panoramic imaging have unified IPM forms.

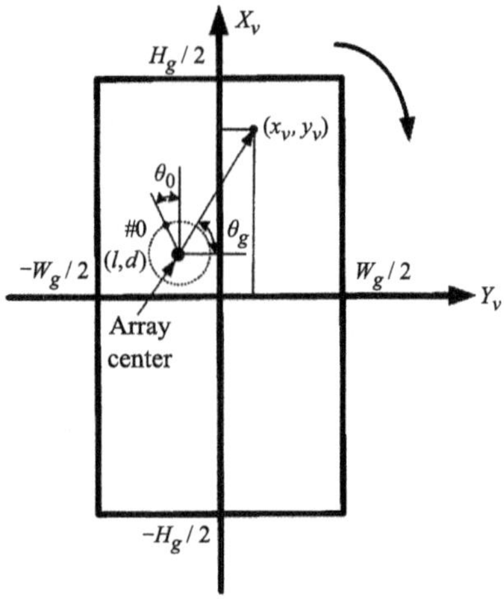


**Fig. 8.4** The illustration of FOV of the panoramic camera in the vehicle coordinate system

## 8.5 The Implementation of the pIPM

### *8.5.1 The Field of View of N Cameras in the Vehicle Coordinate System*

The first step of the implementation of the pIPM is to determine the Field of View (FOV), $x_v \in [-H_g/2, H_g/2]$, $y_v \in [-W_g/2, W_g/2]$, shown in Fig. 8.4.

### *8.5.2 Calculation of Each Interest Point's View Angle in the Vehicle Coordinate System*

For each point in the vehicle coordinate system, we calculate its view angle and determine the corresponding mapping camera. In Fig. 8.4, $X_v O Y_v$ is the vehicle coordinate system, $\theta$ is the view angle, we calculate $\theta_g$ using $x_v$ and $y_v$ and the equation written below

$$\theta_g = \begin{cases} \frac{[1-\mathrm{sgn}(y_v-d_s)(1-\mathrm{sgn}(y_v-d_s))]\pi}{2}, & x_v - l_s = 0 \ (Y_v \text{ axis}), \\ \frac{(1-\mathrm{sgn}(x_v-l_s))\pi}{2}, & y_v - d_s = 0 \ (X_v \text{ axis}), \\ \arctan(\frac{y_v-d_s}{x_v-l_s}), & x_v - l_s > 0 \text{ and } y_v - d_s > 0, \\ \pi + \arctan(\frac{y_v-d_s}{x_v-l_s}), & x_v - l_s < 0 \text{ and } y_v - d_s \neq 0, \\ 2\pi + \arctan(\frac{y_v-d_s}{x_v-l_s}), & x_v - l_s > 0 \text{ and } y_v - d_s < 0, \end{cases} \tag{8.14}$$

where $l_s = \mathrm{sgn}(x_v)l$, $d_s = \mathrm{sgn}(y_v)d$, and where $\mathrm{sgn}(\cdot)$ is the sign function. As a result, we can determine the image plane and $\beta_c$ of $(x_v, y_v)$ given $\theta_g$ by (8.12).

### 8.5.3 The Mapping Relationship Between a 3D On-road Point and a Panoramic Image

From (8.13), we obtain

$$R^{-1}\left\{\begin{bmatrix} x_v \\ y_v \\ z_v \end{bmatrix} - \begin{bmatrix} l' \\ d' \\ h \end{bmatrix}\right\} = t\begin{bmatrix} 1 \\ \frac{\frac{W_p}{2\pi}(\theta_p-\beta_c)+(W_c-2u_0)}{f_u} \\ -\frac{v_p-v_0}{f_v} \end{bmatrix}. \tag{8.15}$$

Using the first line of the above equation and $z_v = 0$, we obtain

$$t = \left[R_{11}^{-1}, R_{12}^{-1}, R_{13}^{-1}\right]\begin{bmatrix} x_v - l' \\ y_v - d' \\ -h \end{bmatrix}. \tag{8.16}$$

Similarly, using the results of the above formula, we obtain

$$\begin{cases} \theta_p = \frac{2\pi}{W_p}\left\{\frac{f_u}{t}[R_{21}^{-1}, R_{22}^{-1}, R_{23}^{-1}]\begin{bmatrix} cx_v-l' \\ y_v-d' \\ -h \end{bmatrix} - (W_c - 2u_0)\right\} + \beta_c, \\ v_p = -\frac{f_v}{t}[R_{31}^{-1}, R_{32}^{-1}, R_{33}^{-1}]\begin{bmatrix} cx_v-l' \\ y_v-d' \\ -h \end{bmatrix} + v_0, \end{cases} \tag{8.17}$$

where $R_{ij}^{-1}$ is the element in the matrix $R^{-1}$ which belongs to the $i$th row and the $j$th column.

Substituting $\theta_g$ from (8.14), $\beta_c$ from (8.13) and $t$ from (8.16) into (8.17), we can obtain the mapping relationship between a panoramic coordinate $(\theta_p, v_p)$ and its corresponding point $(x_v, y_v)$ in the vehicle coordinate system.

### 8.5.4 Image Interpolation in the Vehicle Coordinate System

As we know, $(\theta_p, v_p)$ calculated from $(x_v, y_v, 0)$ could be between pixels. Therefore, we have to calculate the intensity values of each pixel of the panoramic image by interpolating algorithms. Set $(\tilde{\theta}_p, \tilde{v}_p) = (\lfloor\theta_p\rfloor, \lfloor v_p\rfloor)$; here $\lfloor\cdot\rfloor$ is the floor function. Let $p_1$ and $p_2$ denote the distance between $(\theta_p, v_p)$ and $(\tilde{\theta}_p, \tilde{v}_p)$ along $\theta$ and $v$, respectively, as shown in Fig. 8.5. Here, $0 < p_1,\ p_2 < 1$. Therefore, the intensity value of $(x_v, y_v)$ is

$$\begin{aligned} I_v(x_v, y_v) = {} & I_p(\tilde{\theta}_p, \tilde{v}_p)(1-p_1)(1-p_2) + I_p(\tilde{\theta}_p, \tilde{v}_p + 1)(1-p_1)p_2 \\ & + I_p(\tilde{\theta}_p + \Delta\theta_P, \tilde{v}_p)p_1(1-p_2) \\ & + I_p(\tilde{\theta}_p + \Delta\theta_p, \tilde{v}_p + 1)p_1 p_2, \end{aligned} \tag{8.18}$$

**Fig. 8.5** The illustration of non-integer image interpolation

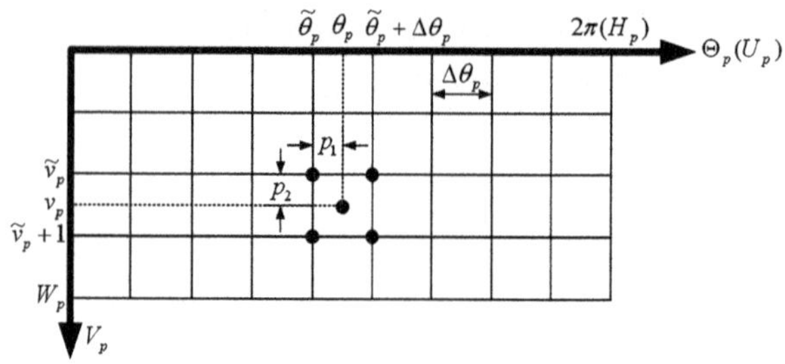

**Fig. 8.6** The results of the pIPM algorithm

where $\Delta\theta_p = \frac{2\pi}{W_p}$. We would like to point out that better interpolation algorithms also can be considered for improving display performance. Figure 8.6 shows the experimental results of the pIPM algorithm.

## 8.6 The Elimination of Wide-Angle Lens' Radial Error

Due to the effect of the number of cameras, we often use a wide-angle lens to increase the angle field of view. However, the wide-angle lens will cause radial distortion; the model is shown below

$$\begin{bmatrix} \tilde{u}_c \\ \tilde{v}_c \end{bmatrix} = \left(1 + \kappa_1 r_d^2 + \kappa_2 r_d^4 + \kappa_5 r_d^6\right) \begin{bmatrix} u_c \\ v_c \end{bmatrix} + dx, \tag{8.19}$$

where $dx = \begin{bmatrix} 2\kappa_3 u_c v_c + \kappa_4 (r_d^2 + 2u_c^2) \\ \kappa_3 (r_d^2 + 2v_c^2) + 2\kappa_4 u_c v_c \end{bmatrix}$, $r_d^2 = u_c^2 + v_c^2$.

**Fig. 8.7** Google global navigation map

## 8.7 Combining Panoramic Images with Electronic Maps

Electronic map services such as Microsoft Virtual Earth and Google Earth can help reduce a driver's load by providing high quality electronic route and turn-to-turn directions. For example, Fig. 8.7 shows the route, generated by Google Earth, around Carnegie Mellon University.

We can further reduce a driver's cognitive load by combining the images captured by the omnidirectional camera with the electronic map in real time. In particular, we perform image analysis to detect surrounding objects such as vehicles and pedestrians, and display the detected objects on the electronic map.

In this approach, we mainly focus on vehicle detection. Our vehicle detection approach includes two basic phases. In the hypothesis generation phase, we first determine the Regions of Interest (ROI) in an image according to lane vanishing points. From the analysis of horizontal and vertical edges in the image, vehicle hypothesis lists are generated for each ROI. In the hypothesis validation phase, we have developed a vehicle validation system by using Support Vector Machine (SVM) and Gabor features. For details we refer to [3, 4]. Figure 8.1 shows the results of vehicle detection in two omnidirectional images.

Let $V_w = [\phi, \gamma, \eta]^T$ denote the coordinates of the host vehicle where $\phi$ and $\gamma$ are provided by an in-vehicle GPS device, and $\eta$ is the direction of vehicle. Let $(x_v(u, v), y_v(u, v))$ denote the coordinate of a detected vehicle, then the latitude and longitude of the detected vehicle can be written as [12]:

$$\begin{bmatrix} \phi_o \\ \gamma_o \end{bmatrix} = \begin{bmatrix} k_1 \cos\eta & -k_1 \sin\eta & \phi \\ k_2 \sin\eta & k_2 \cos\eta & \gamma \end{bmatrix} \begin{bmatrix} x_v(u, v) \\ y_v(u, v) \\ 1 \end{bmatrix}, \tag{8.20}$$

where $k_1$ and $k_2$ are scalar values to put the points into the earth's longitude and latitude coordinate system. Thus we can display the detected vehicle on an electronic map. Figure 8.8 shows the results of displaying the detected vehicles in the two panoramic images as shown in Fig. 8.1 onto the Google Earth map.

(a) (b)

**Fig. 8.8** Mapping from detected objects onto Google Earth map: (**a**) The objects are detected from the top image in Fig. 8.1; (**b**) The objects are detected from the bottom image in Fig. 8.1

## References


1. Cheng, H., Liu, Z., Yang, J.: Learning feature transforms for object detection from panoramic images. In: IEEE International Conference on Multimedia and Expo, pp. 643–648 (2010)
2. Cheng, H., Liu, Z., Zheng, N., Yang, J.: Enhancing a driver's situation awareness using a global view map. In: IEEE International Conference on Multimedia and Expo, pp. 1019–1022 (2007)
3. Cheng, H., Zheng, N., Sun, C.: Boosted gabor features applied to vehicle detection. Pattern Recognit. **1**, 662–666 (2006)
4. Cheng, H., Zheng, N., Sun, C., van de Wetering, H.: Vanishing point and gabor feature based multi-resolution on-road vehicle detection. In: Advances in Neural Networks-ISNN, pp. 46–51 (2006)
5. Cutler, R., Rui, Y., Gupta, A., Cadiz, J., Tashev, I., He, L., Colburn, A., Zhang, Z., Liu, Z., Silverberg, S.: Distributed meetings: A meeting capture and broadcasting system. In: Proc. of ACM international conference on Multimedia, pp. 503–512 (2002)
6. Dale, R., Geldof, S., Prost, J.P.: Using natural language generation in automatic route description. J. Res. Pract. Inform. Technol. **37**(1), 89 (2005)
7. Endsley, M.: Situation awareness global assessment technique (SAGAT). In: Proceedings of the NAECON, pp. 789–795 (1988)
8. Faugeras, O., Luong, Q., Papadopoulo, T.: The Geometry of Multiple Images. MIT press, Cambridge (2001)
9. Fleming, W.: Overview of automotive sensors. IEEE Sens. J. **1**(4), 296–308 (2001)
10. Gandhi, T., Trivedi, M.M.: Dynamic panoramic surround map: motivation and omni video based approach. In: IEEE Computer Society Conference on Computer Vision and Pattern Recognition-Workshops, p. 61 (2005)
11. Gandhi, T., Trivedi, M.M.: Vehicle surround capture: Survey of techniques and a novel omni-video-based approach for dynamic panoramic surround maps. IEEE Trans. Intell. Transp. Syst. **7**(3), 293–308 (2006)
12. Gonzalez, F.G., Andres, R., Deal, D., Goergen, F., Rhodes, M., Roberts, T., Stein, G., Wilson, J., Wong, S.: Black knight: an autonomous vehicle for competition. J. Robot. Syst. **21**(9), 451–460 (2004)

13. Green, P., Levison, W., Paelke, G., Serafin, C.: Preliminary human factors design guidelines for driver information systems. NASA (19980016891) (1995)
14. Lee, J., Forlizzi, J., Hudson, S.: Studying the effectiveness of move: A contextually optimized in-vehicle navigation system. In: Proceedings of ACM CHI, pp. 571–580 (2005)
15. Stutts, J., Reinfurt, D., Staplin, L., Rodgman, E.: The Role of Driver Distraction in Traffic Crashes. AAA Foundation for Traffic Safety, Washington, DC (2001)
16. Szeliski, R.: Computer Vision: Algorithms and Applications. Springer, New York (2010)
17. Szeliski, R., Shum, H.: Creating full view panoramic image mosaics and environment maps. In: Proc. of the 24th Annual Conference on Computer Graphics and Interactive Techniques, pp. 251–258. ACM Press, New York (1997)

# Part IV
# Advanced Vehicle Motion Control

# Chapter 9
# The Lateral Motion Control for Intelligent Vehicles

## 9.1 Introduction

The goals of intelligent transportation systems are to improve the capacity of existing highways, and simplify manual operations under various road conditions. Lane following systems are capable of providing safer and more efficient positioning commands. Hence, the functions of lane following systems are twofold. First, the sensing system must calculate the radius of curvature of the road and the position of the vehicle relative to the road. Second, the lateral controller must not only track the center of the road but also steer the vehicle. In this case, the error between the reference path and the actual path is kept minimal by the control at the cost of both comfort and stability. A typical lane following system consists of four main parts: a lateral controller, a steering wheel, a vehicle and some sensors, as shown in Fig. 9.1. The actual driving response to a road is illustrated in Fig. 9.2.

The rest of this chapter is organized as follows. Section 9.2 reviews the related work. Section 9.3 introduces the proposed mixed lateral control strategy. In Sect. 9.4, we present the relationship between motor pulses and the front wheel lean angle.

## 9.2 Related Work

The vehicle lateral motion control plays a fundamental role in path following [5], Automated Highway Systems (AHS) [2, 3, 9, 11, 12, 15, 18], Advanced Safety Vehicle (ASV) [8], Automated Formation Changes (AFC) [17], and a lot of work has been done. In the AHS, the goal of lateral control is to make vehicles follow road/lane marks under various driving conditions, speeds, loads, road types, and to maintain good comfortability and stability. Toward this end, Peng et al. combined a feedback controller and a feed-forward controller to improve ride quality by using the Frequency-Shaped Linear Quadratic (FSLQ) [12]. The feedback controller uses the FSLQ to improve performance while the feed-forward controller is to generate preview steering commands when the curvature of the coming road is available.

H. Cheng, *Autonomous Intelligent Vehicles*,
Advances in Computer Vision and Pattern Recognition,
DOI 10.1007/978-1-4471-2280-7_9, © Springer-Verlag London Limited 2011

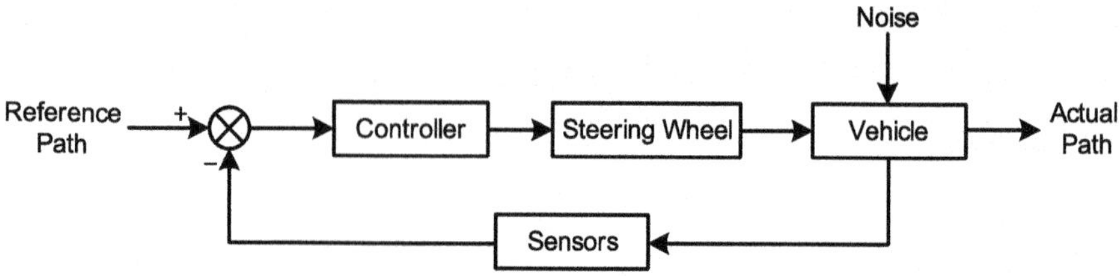


**Fig. 9.1** A typical lateral control framework

**Fig. 9.2** An illustration of actual driving response

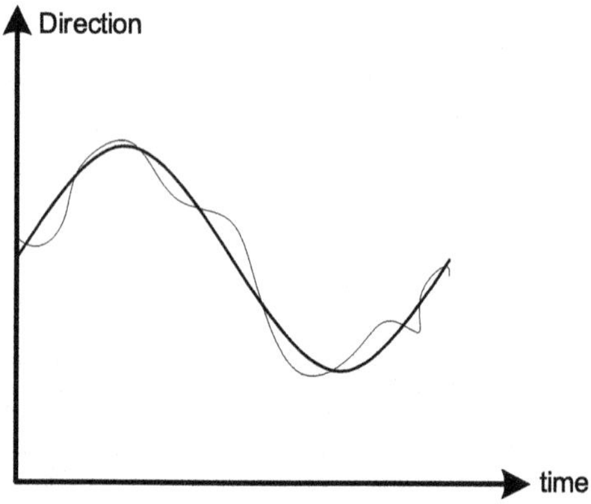


Furthermore, the authors present continuous deterministic preview control consisting of feedback terms and two feed-forward terms [13]. As we know, both safety and passenger comfort are important for buses. Therefore, to obtain superior stability and maneuverability, Matsumoto et al. controlled lateral velocity and yaw rate at the same time by inputting both the force between the front wheels and rear wheels, and the rear steering angle [7]. In Real-time Autonomous Navigator with a Geometric Engine (RANGER), Kelly presented the state space representation of a multi-input multi-output linear system which acts as the perceive–think–act loop for a robot vehicle [6]. To maintain smoothness of the steering system at both high speed and low speed, multiple look-ahead points were introduced to keep tighter turns at low speed. Here, one is used to obtain the deviation from the path while the rest are used to predict the steering angle for feed-forward control. Fraichard et al. proposed the Execution Monitor (EM) whose goal is to follow a given trajectory and respond to unexpected events in real time, thus generating control commands [4].

## 9.3 The Mixed Lateral Control Strategy

To maintain the smoothness of the steering system, different control strategies should be used to control the steering system for linear and curvilinear roads, respectively. Let us first see how a human driver drives a car. When a car enters into

**Table 9.1** The relationship between vehicle velocity, viewpoint angle and focusing-on distance

| | | | | | |
|---|---|---|---|---|---|
| Vehicle velocity (m/s) | 16.667 | 22.222 | 27.778 | 33.333 | 38.889 |
| Angle of viewpoint (°) | 43 | 30 | 20 | 11 | 7 |
| Look-ahead distance (m) | 180 | 300 | 420 | 540 | 640 |
| Look-ahead time (s) | 10.8 | 13.5 | 15.1 | 16.2 | 16.5 |

a curvilinear road region, the driver perceives the curvature of the road by eyes. Afterwards, the driver inputs a proper steering angle thus making a perfect turn according to 'current' conditions. Actually, driverless vehicles should work in a same way. In linear roads, in-car computers calculate look-ahead distance as the input of controllers directly controlling the steering wheel angle of a vehicle. When a control system gives a steering signal, the executive part will respond very quickly and the steering magnitude is very small. By contrast, when the car is entering a curvilinear road, the in-car computer first obtains the radius of the curve and the steering angle, and then generates steering commands. To simulate human driving, we introduce two different control strategies to adapt to different road conditions.

### *9.3.1 Linear Roads*

**1. Determining Look-Ahead Distance** A human driver is focusing on a specified distance before the vehicle when driving. This specified distance is called the look-ahead distance which is related to speed. The relationship among vehicle velocity, viewpoint angle, and focusing-on distance is shown in Table 9.1.

From Table 9.1, we can see that focusing-on distance varies accordingly with both vehicle velocity and angle of viewpoint. Moreover, we have

$$D = 20.88v - 164.01. \tag{9.1}$$

Hence, we repeated experiments many times and got the empirical formulation of look-ahead distance as

$$d_s = D/10. \tag{9.2}$$

**2. Calculating Looking-Ahead Error** The actual path of a driving vehicle could deviate from its reference path due to rough roads, lateral wind, and initial errors. Hence, we need to correct the front wheel lean angle, thus keeping the error between the reference path and the actual path at a minimum. The look-ahead distance error $y_p$ is the distance between point $A$ and $B$ in Fig. 9.3. The slip angle is defined as follows:

$$\theta_s = \arctan\left(\frac{\dot{y}_u}{\dot{x}_u}\right), \tag{9.3}$$

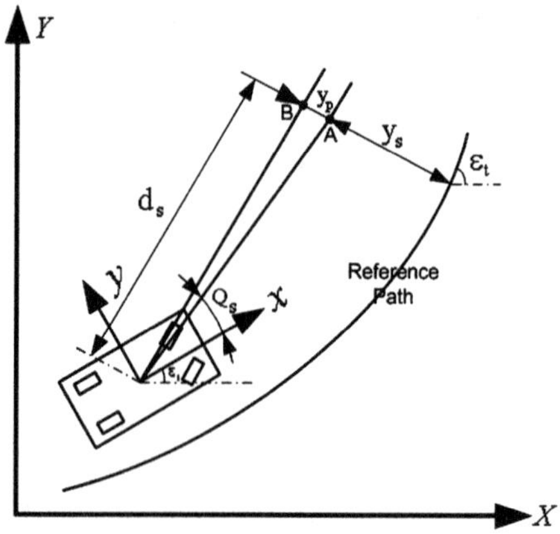


**Fig. 9.3** The geometry model of lateral deviation

where $\dot{y}_u$ and $\dot{x}_u$ are the lateral velocity and longitudinal velocity, respectively. Usually, we assume that $\theta_s$ is negligible since the lateral velocity is much smaller than the longitudinal velocity. As a result, we have [5]

$$\dot{y}_s \approx \dot{y}_u + \dot{x}_u \varepsilon_r + d_s \dot{\varepsilon}_1 + \left(\frac{d_s}{\dot{x}_u}\right) \ddot{y}_u, \tag{9.4}$$

where $\varepsilon_r = \varepsilon_1 - \varepsilon_t$; $\varepsilon_1$ is the angle between the vehicle coordinates and the ground coordinates; $\varepsilon_t$ is the absolute yaw of the reference trajectory in the inertial coordinate frame.

In addition, the driving vehicle has the displacement of lateral slip due to the front wheels rotating. The displacement $y_p$ is then defined in the following form

$$y_p = d_s \tan(\beta), \tag{9.5}$$

where

$$\beta = \frac{1}{2} \arcsin\left(\frac{d_s(\dot{\varepsilon}_1 + \theta_s)}{\dot{x}_v}\right). \tag{9.6}$$

Finally, we calculate the look-ahead distance error as

$$y_e = y_s + y_p. \tag{9.7}$$

### 9.3.2 Curvilinear Roads

When previously considering linear roads, the strategy of look-ahead distance was focusing on a fixed point. In other words, we only considered the error between the reference path and the actual path at a specified point. Obviously, this strategy ignores other geometry information of a road in front of the vehicle, such as the orientation and curvature. As a result, the performance of the controller degrades. In this section, we will incorporate more road geometric information into the controller.

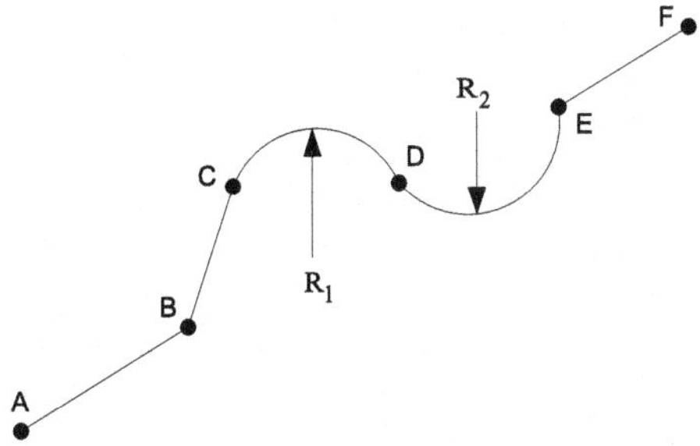


**Fig. 9.4** The geometry model of lateral deviation

**1. Existing Shape Representation** Assume that object contours consist of lines and arcs, where corners are intersection points between lines/arcs and lines/arcs, as shown in Fig. 9.4. The shape representation of a contour is to keep the number of both lines and arcs at a minimum by segmenting approaches. There are two types of contour segmenting techniques: the first one is direct [14, 19], the other is indirect [1, 10]. The direct approaches are to segment object shapes using point sets of object contours [14, 19], while the indirect approaches are to formulate the problem of segmenting contours into the characteristic functions of the contours [1, 10].

*The Direct Approaches*: Let $P_s$ and $P_e$ denote the start point and end point of a contour, respectively. First, we calculate the distance $d_i$ between point $P_c$ and line $P_sP_e$. If $d_{\max} = \max_i\{d_i\} < \varepsilon_0$ ($\varepsilon_0$ is a small constant), the contour $P_sP_e$ is a line. Second, if $d_{\max} \geq \varepsilon_0$, we will continue to segment the contour until $d_{\max} < \varepsilon_0$. Finally, the direct approaches generate some subsets of points which approximate lines. The advantages of the direct approaches are as follows: (i) The implementation of these approaches is simple; (ii) They can achieve very high precision of shape representation by adjusting $\varepsilon_0$. However, the disadvantages of the direct approaches are as follows: (i) They have high computing burden due to large amount of distance computation between points and lines; (ii) The value of $\varepsilon_0$ greatly affects the result of contour segmentation; (iii) The results of segmenting contours are only lines, but not circles/arcs.

*The Indirect Approaches*: The curvature extreme approaches are typical indirect approaches. In this approach, the point $P_i$ with curvature $C_i$ larger than threshold $C_T$ is a contour corner. We can see that: (i) It is convenient to calculate the curvature once for each point; (ii) Segmented contours are invariant with respect to rotation. Unfortunately, the indirect approaches are very sensitive to noise. Moreover, the curve extreme corresponds to contour corners, not tangent points. Toward this end, we propose a segmenting approach of contours based on the sum of ideal contours.

**2. The Proposed Segmenting Approach of Contours** Let us discuss the real contour in Fig. 9.4. Assume that the contour consists of lines and arcs. Given the types of segmented contours and the positions of all the corners and tangent points, we can obtain the curves of the curvature and its sum, shown in Fig. 9.5. In Fig. 9.5, the curvature values of line $AB$, $BC$, $EF$ are 0, and the curvature values of arc $CD$

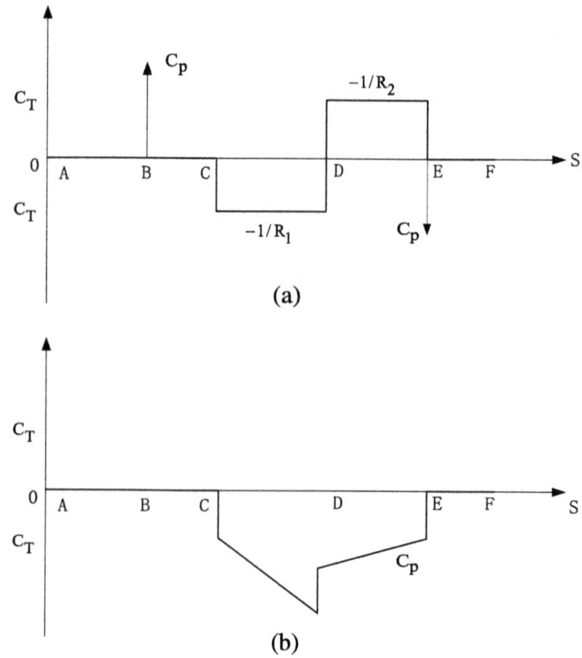


**Fig. 9.5** Ideal contours: (**a**) curvatures, (**b**) the sum of curvatures

and $DE$ are $-1/R_1$ and $1/R_2$, respectively. From Fig. 9.5, we can see that:

1. The corners of contours correspond to the pulses of curvature $C_P$ which is larger than $C_T$.
2. There does not exist a corner between two neighboring corners, but there could exist a tangent point. The contour segment between two corners is either a line or an arc if there is no tangent point. Otherwise, the contour segment consists of a line and an arc which are tangent.
3. A line contour segment without a tangent point between two neighboring corners must agree in two aspects. First, the curvatures of all the points are 0. Second, the sum of curvatures of all the points is 0.
4. A tangent point between two neighboring corners has the following properties. The curvature change of the tangent point corresponds to a step wave. At the same time, the sum of its curvature changes suddenly.
5. If a contour segment satisfies Condition 3, it is a line. Otherwise, it is an arc.
6. The orientations of arc contours can be determined by the signs of the curvatures of arcs. Correspondingly, the signs of the curvatures skew can determine its orientation.

Using the above properties, we can segment a contour only consisting of lines and arcs. However, real contours could be affected by a large amount of random noise. Figure 9.6 shows the curvatures of a real contour. We can see that: (i) the curvatures of a real contour are not horizontal but curved. Also, the pulse at the corner becomes local maximum/minimum in real contours; (ii) It is difficult to distinguish

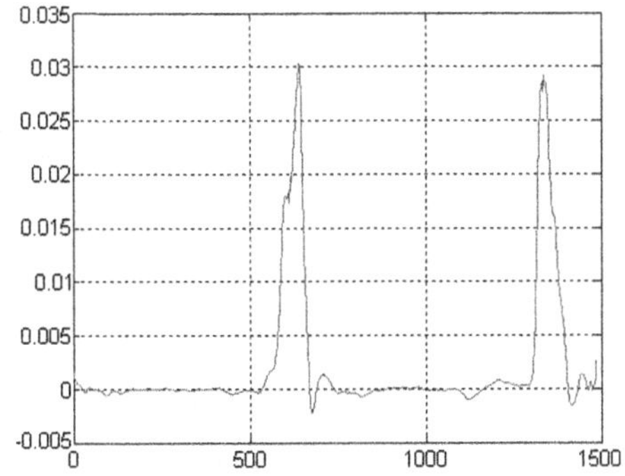


**Fig. 9.6** The curvature of a real contour

the curvatures of lines and arcs since the curvatures of contours with a large radius are greatly affected by noise.

Now we discuss the curvatures of roads. The values of sampling points consist of two items, real data $r(s)$ and random noise $\delta$. The curvatures of lines and arcs are 0 and $\pm 1/R$, respectively.

Consequently, the curvature of the real line is a random function, $C_l(s) = \delta_l$. Similarly, that of the real arc is described as $\pm 1/R + \delta_c$. From the statistical properties of random errors, the sum of random errors is zero, and we have

$$\sum_{c=1}^{N} C_c(s) = \pm \sum_{c=1}^{N} \frac{1}{R} + \sum_{c=1}^{N} \delta_c = \pm \frac{N}{R}, \qquad \sum_{l=1}^{N} C_l(s) = \sum \delta_l = 0, \tag{9.8}$$

where $N$ is the number of points on the contour.

### *9.3.3 Calculating the Radius of an Arc*

The ideal equation of a circle is given in the following form

$$(x - x_0)^2 + (y - y_0)^2 = r^2, \tag{9.9}$$

where $(x_0, y_0)$ is the center of the circle. It has another form as follows:

$$x^2 + y^2 - 2x_0 x - 2y_0 y + (x_0^2 + y_0^2 - r^2) = 0. \tag{9.10}$$

Given observed points $p_i(x_i, y_i)$, $i = 1, 2, 3, \ldots, N$, we substitute them into (9.9), and obtain the error function

$$\Delta_i = x_i^2 + y_i^2 - 2x_0 x_i - 2y_0 y_i + (x_0^2 + y_0^2 - r^2). \tag{9.11}$$

From least-mean-square algorithms, we can obtain the radius $r$ of the ideal circle by minimizing $\sum \Delta_i^2$. Defining $f(x_0, y_0, x_1, y_1, x_2, y_2, \ldots, x_N, y_N, r) = \sum_{i=1}^{N} \Delta_i^2$,

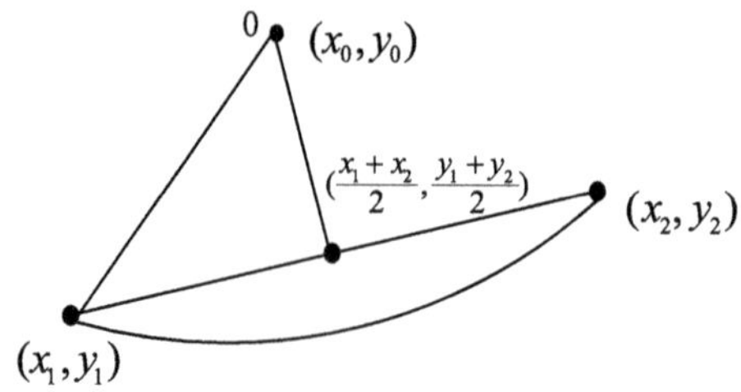


**Fig. 9.7** The geometric relationship when solving for the radius of a circle

we have

$$\frac{df}{dr} = 0. \tag{9.12}$$

In Fig. 9.7, we define the equation of the line $OA$ as $y = kx + b$. It is easy to obtain $k = -\frac{x_2-x_1}{y_2-y_1}$ and $b = \frac{y_2^2-y_1^2+x_2^2-x_1^2}{2(y_2-y_1)}$. Then we can obtain the solution of $(x_0, y_0)$ by using two conditions. First, when $y_1 \neq y_2$,

$$\begin{cases} x_0 = \frac{\sum_{i=1}^{N}[2b(y_1-y_i)+(x_i^2-x_1^2)+(y_i^2-y_1^2)](y_i-y_1)}{2\sum_{i=1}^{N}[(x_1-x_i)+k(y_1-y_i)]^2}, \\ y_0 = kx_0 + b, \end{cases} \tag{9.13}$$

when $y_1 = y_2$,

$$\begin{cases} x_0 = \frac{x_1+x_2}{2}, \\ y_0 = \frac{\sum_{i=1}^{N}[(x_i^2-x_1^2)-2x_0(x_i-x_1)+(y_i^2-y_1^2)](y_i-y_1)}{2\sum_{i=1}^{N}(y_i-y_1)^2}. \end{cases} \tag{9.14}$$

Now, the radius of the circle is calculated from the distance between $(x_0, y_0)$ and $(x_i, y_i)$

$$r = \sqrt{(x_i - x_0)^2 + (y_i - y_0)^2}. \tag{9.15}$$

### 9.3.4 The Algorithm Flow

1. Smooth sampled data, and calculate the curvatures of each sampling point, thus yielding the curve $\zeta - n$. The curvature at point $(x, y)$ is represented by

$$k(x, y) = \frac{\dot{x}\ddot{y} - \dot{y}\ddot{x}}{(\dot{x}^2 + \dot{y}^2)^{3/2}}, \tag{9.16}$$

where $\dot{x} = dx/dt$, $\ddot{x} = d^2x/dt^2$, $\dot{y} = dy/dt$, $\ddot{y} = d^2y/dt^2$. Furthermore, its discrete form is

$$\dot{x}_k = x_{k+1} - x_{k-1}, \qquad \ddot{x}_k = x_{k+1} + x_{k-1} - 2x_k. \tag{9.17}$$

2. Difference operations are sensitive to noise. Therefore, we need to smooth the curvature of curves before seeking the extreme of curvature. In practice, the Gaussian filters can remove the effect of random noise. As a result, the Gaussian filters are used to smooth the curvature.

   The $1D$ Gaussian smoothing filter is given by

$$h(t,\sigma)=\frac{1}{\sqrt{2\pi}\sigma}e^{-\frac{t^2}{2\sigma^2}}. \tag{9.18}$$

   The smoothed curve is

$$\begin{cases} X(t,\sigma)=x(t)*h(t,\sigma), \\ Y(t,\sigma)=y(t)*h(t,\sigma), \end{cases} \tag{9.19}$$

   where $\sigma$ is the standard deviation and $*$ is the convolution operator.
3. Seek the local extreme of the curvature which corresponds to the corners of real contours.
4. Merge the corners whose distance is smaller than $\sigma$, and keep the corners $N_1$ with bigger curvature.
5. Accumulate the curvature between two neighboring corners, thus yielding the curve of accumulated curvature.
6. Calculate the intersection point of the curve of accumulated curvature between the two neighboring corners which correspond to the tangent points $N_2$ of the contour of the trace.
7. Calculate the final segmenting point set $N=N_1\cup N_2$.
8. Make a decision on contour types, either lines or arcs, from the curvature and accumulated curvature of contours.
9. Calculate the radius $r$ between two segmenting points, and fit the shapes of each road segment.

To validate the proposed approach, we collected the road data using DGPS by the Springrobot platform, as shown in Fig. 9.8. First, we filter the road curve using (9.19) (shown in Fig. 9.8(b)), while the blue solid line is the result of the filtered curve, and ‘o’ denotes the original points. For better illustration, we take one point within each contour segment with 0.5 m. Furthermore, we obtain corner points (red ‘o’ in Fig. 9.8(c)) of a road contour. Finally, we generate a fitted contour in Fig. 9.8(d). To have a closer look at the performance of curve fitting, we list the fitting errors of some sampling points in Table 9.2.

## 9.4 The Relationship Between Motor Pulses and the Front Wheel Lean Angle

To obtain the relationship between motor pulses and the angle of the frontal wheel, we give pulse commands to servomotor, and then measure the angle between the

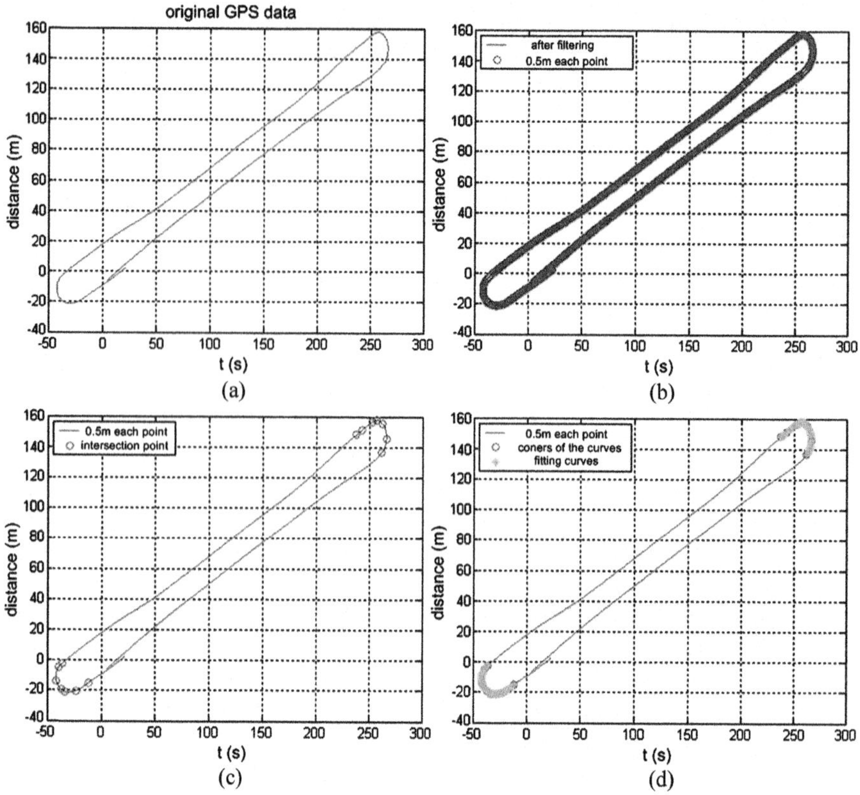


Fig. 9.8 Road curve fitting

Fig. 9.9 The relationship between motor pulses and the frontal wheel lean angle

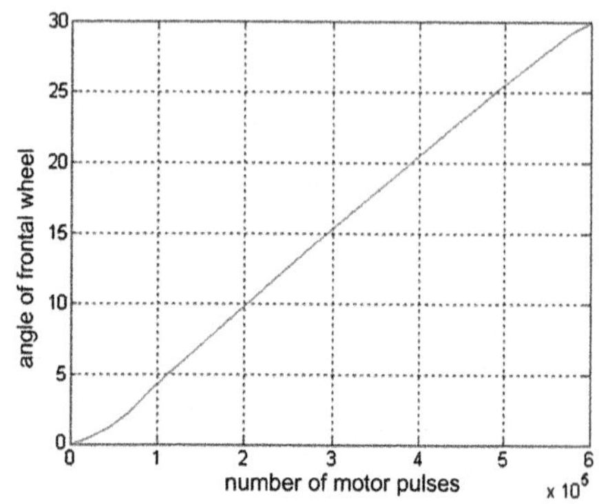


frontal wheel and the central line of the vehicle. Similarly, we can get the relationship between motor pulses and the angle of steering wheel. The data is shown in Table 9.3.

**Table 9.2** Error of the road curve fitting

| Point index | Error (m) | Point index | Error (m) | Point index | Error (m) |
|---|---|---|---|---|---|
| 588 | 0 | 621 | −0.022514 | 654 | −0.043589 |
| 589 | −0.012631 | 622 | −0.039874 | 655 | −0.053452 |
| 590 | −0.020484 | 623 | −0.052511 | 656 | −0.056682 |
| 591 | −0.024201 | 624 | −0.060143 | 657 | −0.054189 |
| 592 | −0.024525 | 625 | −0.062779 | 658 | −0.046865 |
| 593 | −0.022203 | 626 | −0.06039 | 659 | −0.035606 |
| 594 | −0.017965 | 627 | −0.052993 | 660 | −0.02133 |
| 595 | −0.012483 | 628 | −0.040492 | 661 | −0.0049879 |
| 596 | −0.0064056 | 629 | −0.022922 | 662 | 0.012451 |
| 597 | −0.00016625 | 630 | 0 | 663 | 0.029959 |
| 598 | 0.0058921 | 631 | 0.0051631 | 664 | 0.046507 |
| 599 | 0.011541 | 632 | 0.0069396 | 665 | 0.061063 |
| 600 | 0.016601 | 633 | 0.0064731 | 666 | 0.072614 |
| 601 | 0.021038 | 634 | 0.0046559 | 667 | 0.080203 |
| 602 | 0.024897 | 635 | 0.0022215 | 668 | 0.082944 |
| 603 | 0.028119 | 636 | −0.00025257 | 669 | 0.080041 |
| 604 | 0.03077 | 637 | −0.0023255 | 670 | 0.070818 |
| 605 | 0.032688 | 638 | −0.0036638 | 671 | 0.054699 |
| 606 | 0.033284 | 639 | −0.0040793 | 672 | 0 |
| 607 | 0.031133 | 640 | −0.0035323 | 673 | 0 |
| 608 | 0.023164 | 641 | −0.0022453 | 674 | 0.0020647 |
| 609 | −2.8422e−014 | 642 | −0.00074659 | 675 | 0.0032209 |
| 610 | −0.1623 | 643 | 0 | 676 | 0.0035146 |
| 611 | −0.38312 | 644 | −0.0077284 | 677 | 0.0030564 |
| 612 | 0.56721 | 645 | −0.0097033 | 678 | 0.002007 |
| 613 | 0.3719 | 646 | −0.0073691 | 679 | 0.00056412 |
| 614 | 0.26257 | 647 | −0.0023915 | 680 | −0.0010431 |
| 615 | 0.19258 | 648 | 0.0034642 | 681 | −0.0025696 |
| 616 | 0.13888 | 649 | 0.0084324 | 682 | −0.0037593 |
| 617 | 0.095585 | 650 | 0.010715 | 683 | −0.0043517 |
| 618 | 0.058418 | 651 | 0.008503 | 684 | −0.0040855 |
| 619 | 0.026803 | 652 | 0 | 685 | −0.0027133 |
| 620 | −0.00028067 | 653 | −0.026126 | 686 | −2.8422e−014 |

From Fig. 9.9, we can obtain the regression function

$$\xi = 5.18 \times 10^{-5} P, \tag{9.20}$$

where $\xi$ is the angle of frontal wheel, and $P$ is the number of motor pulses.

We would like to point out that a fuzzy controller is used as the lateral controller. For the details, we refer to [16].

**Table 9.3** The relationship between the angle of steering wheel, motor pulses, and the angle of frontal wheel

| Sequence | Name | | |
|---|---|---|---|
| | Angle of steering wheel | Motor pulses | Angle of frontal wheel |
| 1 | 0 | 0 | 0 |
| 2 | 20 | 22222 | 0.474122 |
| 3 | 40 | 44444 | 1.173539 |
| 4 | 60 | 66667 | 2.276610 |
| 5 | 80 | 88889 | 3.622666 |
| 6 | 100 | 111111 | 4.913494 |
| 7 | 120 | 133333 | 6.100710 |
| 8 | 140 | 155556 | 7.361193 |
| 9 | 160 | 177778 | 8.577056 |
| 10 | 180 | 200000 | 9.769596 |
| 11 | 200 | 222222 | 11.01529 |
| 12 | 220 | 244444 | 12.24955 |
| 13 | 240 | 266667 | 13.47108 |
| 14 | 260 | 288889 | 14.70033 |
| 15 | 280 | 311111 | 15.91294 |
| 16 | 300 | 333333 | 17.0687 |
| 17 | 320 | 355556 | 18.22439 |
| 18 | 340 | 377778 | 19.37022 |
| 19 | 360 | 400000 | 20.50419 |
| 20 | 380 | 422222 | 21.63254 |
| 21 | 400 | 444444 | 22.74814 |
| 22 | 420 | 466667 | 23.85487 |
| 23 | 440 | 488889 | 24.94044 |
| 24 | 460 | 511111 | 26.01698 |
| 25 | 480 | 533333 | 27.05728 |
| 26 | 500 | 555556 | 28.1043 |
| 27 | 520 | 577778 | 29.15082 |
| 28 | 540 | 600000 | 29.93288 |

## References


1. Ansari, N., Delp, E.J.: On detecting dominant points. Pattern Recognit. **24**, 441–451 (1991)
2. Aso, M., Suzuki, T.: Automated steering control for the intelligent multimode transit system. In: Proc. of the IEEE International Conference on Intelligent Vehicles Symposium, pp. 590–595 (2000)
3. Bergese, C., Braun, A., Porta, E.: Inside CHAUFFEUR. In: The 6th ITS World Congress, Toronto, Canada (1999)
4. Fraichard, T., Garnier, P.: Fuzzy control to drive car-like vehicles. Robot. Auton. Syst. **34**(1), 1–22 (2001)

5. Hayakawa, Y., White, R., Kimura, T., Naitou, G.: Driver oriented path following in ITS. In: Proc. of the IEEE/ASME International Conference on Advanced Intelligent Mechatronics (2003)
6. Kelly, A.: A Feedforward Control Approach to the Local Navigation Problem for Autonomous Vehicles. Citeseer, Pennsylvania (1994)
7. Matsumoto, S., Yamaguchi, H., Hano, S., Inoue, H.: Vehicle Turning Behavior Control System (1992). Google Patents
8. Matsumoto, S., Yasuda, T., Kimura, T., Takahama, T., Toyota, H.: Development of the Nissan ASV-2 (2001). Nissan Motor Co., LTD Paper
9. O'Brien, R., Iglesias, P., Urban, T.: Vehicle lateral control for automated highway systems. IEEE Trans. Control Syst. Technol. **4**(3), 266–273 (1996)
10. Pei, S.C., Lin, C.N.: The detection of dominant points on digital curves by scale-space filtering. Pattern Recognit. **25**(11), 1307–1314 (1992)
11. Peng, H., Hessburg, T., Tomizuka, M., Zhang, W.B., Lin, Y., Devlin, P., Shladover, S.E., Arai, A.: A theoretical and experimental study on vehicle lateral control. In: American Control Conference. IEEE, New York (1992)
12. Peng, H., Tomizuka, M.: Vehicle lateral control for highway automation. In: American Control Conference. IEEE, New York (1992)
13. Peng, H., Tomizuka, M.: Preview control for vehicle lateral guidance in highway automation. In: American Control Conference. IEEE, New York (1993)
14. Rattarangsi, A., Chin, R.T.: Scale-based detection of corners of planar curves. IEEE Trans. Pattern Anal. Mach. Intell. **14**(4), 430–449 (1992)
15. Tamura, K., Furukawa, Y.: Autonomous vehicle control system of ICVS City Pal: electrical tow-bar function. In: Proc. of the IEEE International Conference on Intelligent Vehicles Symposium (2000)
16. Tang, J.: Fuzzy controller design and integrated navigation for intelligent vehicles. Master's Thesis, Xi'an Jiaotong University (2005)
17. Tsugawa, S., Kato, S., Tokuda, K., Matsui, T., Fujii, H.: A cooperative driving system with automated vehicles and inter-vehicle communications in Demo 2000. In: Proc. of the IEEE International Conference on Intelligent Transportation Systems (2001)
18. White, R., Tomizuka, M.: Autonomous following lateral control of heavy vehicles using laser scanning radar. In: Proc. of the American Control Conference (2001)
19. Wu, J.S., Leou, J.I.N.J.: New polygonal approximation schemes for object shape representation. Pattern Recognit. **26**(4), 471–484 (1993)

# Chapter 10
# Longitudinal Motion Control for Intelligent Vehicles

## 10.1 Introduction

From a system viewpoint, driving control tasks are to give pulse commands to throttles, brakes and steer wheels to vehicle body, thus implementing vehicle state change by vehicle dynamics. As we know, lateral road departures and longitudinal collisions are the main sources of traffic accidents. Toward this end, the goal of longitudinal control is to control a vehicle according to its relative position with respect to either the lead vehicle or obstacles. Many approaches have been proposed to follow the lead vehicle since the 1960s [3, 5, 8, 9].

The main longitudinal control approaches include PID approaches, mixed integer linear programming [3], backing control [10, 11], fuzzy control [12, 13], and neural control [6, 7]. As the seminal work, the ALVINN used a single hidden layer back-propagation network to control NAVLAB by directly inputting a $30 \times 30$ unit $2D$ image after training, thus keeping the vehicle on the road [6, 7]. In the early stages, people selected either lateral control or longitudinal control for different applications, not attempting to integrate the lateral and longitudinal control. Actually, this is the basic assumption of the PATH control system [8]. In many applications of intelligent vehicles, lateral control and longitudinal control are closely related. Hence, Li et al. investigated tire/road friction modeling for integrated lateral control and longitudinal control [4]. Moreover, many controller strategies incorporated a modeling strategy of human driving behavior. As an example, Kim et al. proposed using Piecewise Polynomial (PWP) model to represent the mapping from the driver's sensing information to the driving operations [3].

Figure 10.1 illustrates the framework of the control system. This framework consists of a controller group, an executive module, feedback sensors, and a vehicle body.

The rest of this chapter is organized as follows. Section 10.2 introduces the system identification in the vehicle longitudinal control. Section 10.3 presents the proposed controller. Section 10.4 validates the proposed controller.

H. Cheng, *Autonomous Intelligent Vehicles*,
Advances in Computer Vision and Pattern Recognition,
DOI 10.1007/978-1-4471-2280-7_10, 

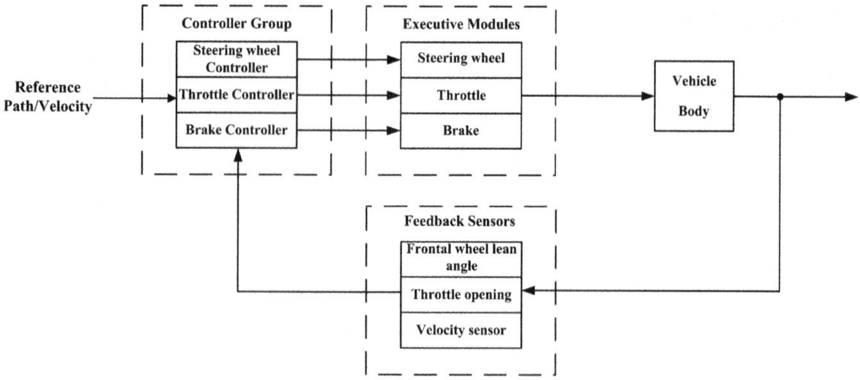


**Fig. 10.1** The framework of a control system

## 10.2 System Identification in Vehicle Longitudinal Control

To control a vehicle better, it is necessary for estimating the dynamical model of the vehicle. The commonly-used dynamical models are described as

$$\text{First order systems:} \quad H(s) = \frac{K_0}{T_0 s + 1}, \tag{10.1}$$

$$\text{First-order lag systems:} \quad H(s) = \frac{K_0}{T_0 s + 1} e^{-\tau s}, \tag{10.2}$$

$$\text{Second order systems:} \quad H(s) = \frac{K_0}{(T_1 s + 1)(T_2 s + 1)}, \tag{10.3}$$

$$\text{Second-order lag systems:} \quad H(s) = \frac{K_0}{(T_1 s + 1)(T_2 s + 1)} e^{-\tau s}, \tag{10.4}$$

where $K_0, T_0/T_1/T_2$, and $\tau$ are the magnifying coefficient, time constants and the time lag, respectively. Usually, we can identify those parameters by the curve of step response. In practice, either first-order systems in (10.1) or first-order lag systems can approximate the real system very well. We briefly discuss how to select a system model and its parameters below.

### *10.2.1 The First-Order Systems*

Given a step signal $x_0$, we can get its stable output $y(\infty)$ from Fig. 10.2(a). Afterwards, we can calculate both $K_0$ and $T_0$ according to the following steps.

- Calculate $K_0$ by

$$K_0 = \frac{y(\infty)}{x_0}. \tag{10.5}$$

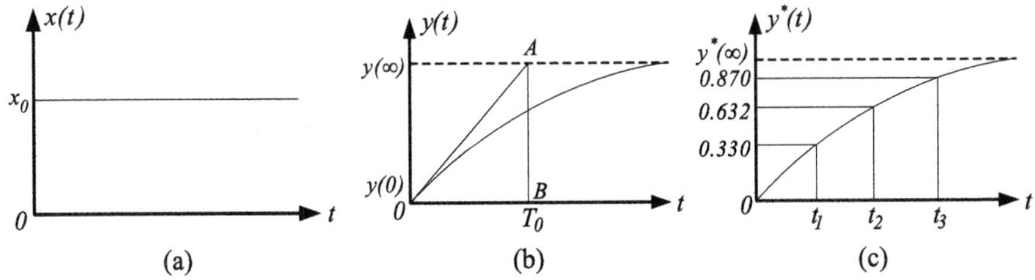


**Fig. 10.2** The step response curve: (**a**) the input function $x(t)$; (**b**) the response function $y(t)$ of $x(t)$; (**c**) the normalized response function $y^*(t)$ of $x(t)$

- To calculate $T_0$, first normalize the response of a step signal shown in Fig. 10.2(b) by

$$y^*(t) = \frac{y(t)}{y(\infty)}, \tag{10.6}$$

and get the solution of $y^*(t)$ (shown in Fig. 10.2(c)) as

$$y^*(t) = 1 - e^{-t/T_0}. \tag{10.7}$$

Therefore, we get

$$T_0 = \frac{-t}{\ln(1 - y^*(t))}. \tag{10.8}$$

Now, we select two points from the normalized curve, namely $y^*(t_1) = 0.333$ and $y^*(t_2) = 0.632$, and calculate its corresponding time constants

$$\begin{cases} T_1 = \frac{-t_1}{\ln(1-y^*(t_1))} = 2.5t_1, \\ T_2 = \frac{-t_2}{\ln(1-y^*(t_2))} = t_2. \end{cases} \tag{10.9}$$

If $T_1 \approx T_2$, we obtain $T_0 = \frac{T_1+T_2}{2}$. However, when $(T_1 - T_2) \geq \varepsilon$ (a constant), we will adopt either second-order systems or first-order lag systems.

We can evaluate how the first-order system function approximates the normalized $y^*(t)$ at $t_3 = T_0/2$ and $t_4 = 2T_0$. From (10.7), we have

$$\begin{cases} y^*(t_3) = 1 - e^{-\frac{T_0}{2T_0}} = 0.39, & t_3 = T_0/2; \\ y^*(t_4) = 1 - e^{-\frac{2T_0}{T_0}} = 0.87, & t_4 = 2T_0. \end{cases} \tag{10.10}$$

If the values of $y^*(t)$ from Fig. 10.2 at time $t_3$ and $t_4$ are remarkably different from $y^*(t_3)$ and $y^*(t_4)$ in (10.10), it means large error. As a result, we have to select another system function, such as a first-order lag system function.

### 10.2.2 First-Order Lag Systems

Similar to the first-order systems, we first normalize $y(t)$ into $y^*(t)$ by

$$y^*(t) = \frac{y(t)}{y(\infty)}. \tag{10.11}$$

Therefore, the solution $y^*(t)$ is then

$$y^*(t) = \begin{cases} 0, & t < \tau; \\ 1 - e^{-\frac{t-\tau}{T_0}}, & t \geq \tau. \end{cases} \tag{10.12}$$

Similar to the first-order systems, we take different values of $y^*(t_1)$ and $y^*(t_2)$ at times $t_1$ and $t_2$ in Fig. 10.2. Afterwards, we can calculate $T_0$ and $\tau$ by solving

$$\begin{cases} y^*(t_1) = 1 - e^{-\frac{t_1-\tau}{T_0}}, \\ y^*(t_2) = 1 - e^{-\frac{t_2-\tau}{T_0}}. \end{cases} \tag{10.13}$$

Assuming $t_2 > t_1 > \tau$ in (10.13), we take logarithms and obtain

$$\begin{cases} \ln(1 - y^*(t_1)) = -\frac{t_1-\tau}{T_0}, \\ \ln(1 - y^*(t_2)) = -\frac{t_2-\tau}{T_0}. \end{cases} \tag{10.14}$$

Hence, from (10.14), we have

$$\begin{cases} T_0 = \frac{t_2-t_1}{\ln(1-y^*(t_1))-\ln(1-y^*(t_2))}, \\ \tau = \frac{t_2\ln(1-y^*(t_1))-t_1\ln(1-y^*(t_2))}{\ln(1-y^*(t_1))-\ln(1-y^*(t_2))}. \end{cases} \tag{10.15}$$

For computing convenience, we take $y^*(t_1) = 0.390$, $y^*(t_2) = 0.632$, and then we have

$$\begin{cases} T_0 = 2(t_2 - t_1), \\ \tau = 2t_1 - t_2. \end{cases} \tag{10.16}$$

After obtaining $T_0$ and $\tau$, we will check $y^*(t)$ at times $t_3$, $t_4$, and $t_5$:

$$\begin{cases} y^*(t_3) = 0, & t_3 < \tau; \\ y^*(t_4) = 0.55, & t_4 = 0.8T_0 + \tau; \\ y^*(t_5) = 0.865, & t_5 = 2T_0 + \tau. \end{cases} \tag{10.17}$$

If the values of the normalized curve at times $t_3$, $t_4$ and $t_5$ are remarkably different from the above values, we could further validate second-order systems. For simplifying our exposition, we do not discuss this validation further. For the identification of a second-order system, we refer to [1].

Fig. 10.3 The brake system

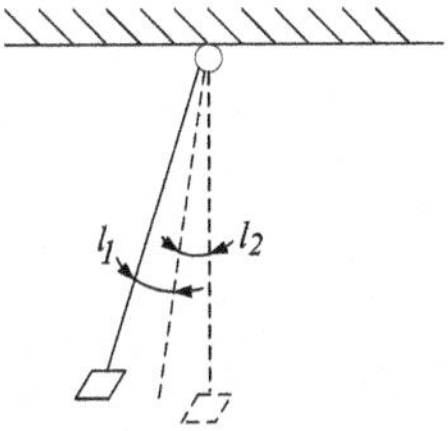


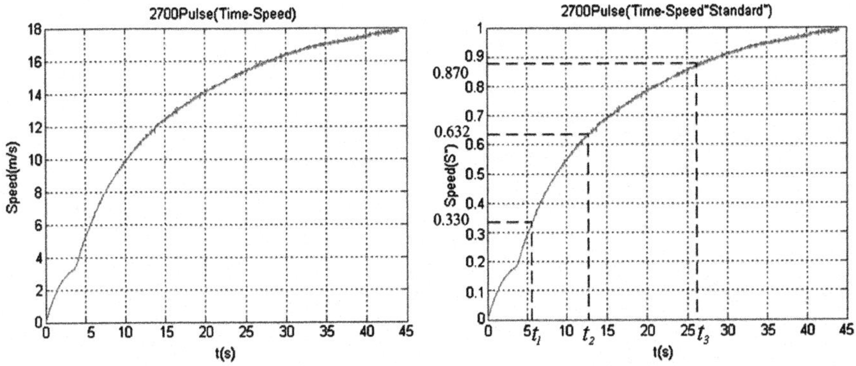


(a) Before normalization (b) After normalization

**Fig. 10.4** The response curve of a step signal

### *10.2.3 Identification of Our Vehicle System*

In this section, we explain how to identify the velocity model. Our test field is a flat road whose length is 3 km. Figure 10.3 shows the brake system, where $l_1$ is the dead zone and $l_2$ is the effective range. In our experiment, we input 1800 pulses before vehicle's acceleration, and get $y(\infty) = 18$ after inputting 2700 pulses (shown in Fig. 10.4).

**1. The First-Order System Assumption** The magnifying coefficient $K_0$ is calculated by (10.5) and is

$$K_0 = \frac{y(\infty)}{x_0} = \frac{18}{2700 - 1800} = 0.02. \tag{10.18}$$

We take two points from the normalized curve in Fig. 10.4, namely $y^*(t_1) = 0.330$ and $y^*(t_2) = 0.632$, and then calculate the time constants

$$\begin{cases} T_1 = \frac{-t_1}{\ln(1-0.632)} = 2.5t_1, \\ T_2 = \frac{-t_2}{\ln(1-0.330)} = t_2. \end{cases} \tag{10.19}$$

Since $t_1 = 5.6$ s and $t_2 = 12.7$ s are observed in our experiment, $T_1 \approx T_2$. As a result, $T_0 = \frac{T_1+T_2}{2} = 13.35$ s.

Now we obtain the first-order system

$$H(s) = \frac{0.02}{13.35s + 1}, \tag{10.20}$$

and validate the normalized values of step response at times $t_3 = T_0/2$ and $t_4 = 2T_0$. From (10.7), we have

$$\begin{cases} y^*(T_0/2) = 1 - e^{-\frac{T_0}{2T_0}} = 0.39, \\ y^*(2T_0) = 1 - e^{-\frac{2T_0}{T_0}} = 0.87. \end{cases} \tag{10.21}$$

The corresponding values of normalized curve of step response at times $t_3$ and $t_4$ are 0.405 and 0.833, respectively. As a result, the error between the actual and the ideal system is very small.

**2. Validating the First-Order Lag Assumption** In Fig. 10.4, there exists a sudden slope change, which means time lag. According to the curve of Fig. 10.4, we have $y^*(t_1) = 0.390$ and $y^*(t_2) = 0.632$, where $t_1 = 6.6$ s, $t_2 = 12.7$ s; hence, we get $T_0$ and $\tau$ by (10.16)

$$\begin{cases} T_0 = 2(t_2 - t_1) = 12.2, \\ \tau = 2t_1 - t_2 = 0.5. \end{cases} \tag{10.22}$$

That is,

$$H(s) = \frac{0.02}{12.2s + 1} e^{-0.5s}. \tag{10.23}$$

Now, we take the values of the normalized curve at times $t_3 = 0.8T_0 + \tau$ and $t_4 = 2T_0 + \tau$ to validate the model

$$\begin{cases} y'(t_3) = 0.55, & t_3 = 0.8T_0 + \tau; \\ y'(t_4) = 0.865, & t_4 = 2T_0 + \tau. \end{cases} \tag{10.24}$$

The values of the normalized curve at times $t_3$ and $t_4$ are 0.55 and 0.8535, respectively. As a result, the error between the ideal first-order lag system and the Springrobot system model is very small.

**3. Validating Second-Order Assumption** According to the curve of Fig. 10.4, we have $y^*(t_1) = 0.4$ and $y^*(t_2) = 0.8$, where $t_1 = 6.8$ s and $t_2 = 21.225$ s. Hence, we get $T_1$ and $T_2$ [1] as

$$\begin{cases} T_1 + T_2 \approx \frac{t_1 + t_2}{2.16} \approx 12.975, \\ \frac{T_1 * T_2}{(T_1 + T_2)^2} \approx 1.74\frac{t_1}{t_2} - 0.55 \approx 0.00746. \end{cases} \tag{10.25}$$

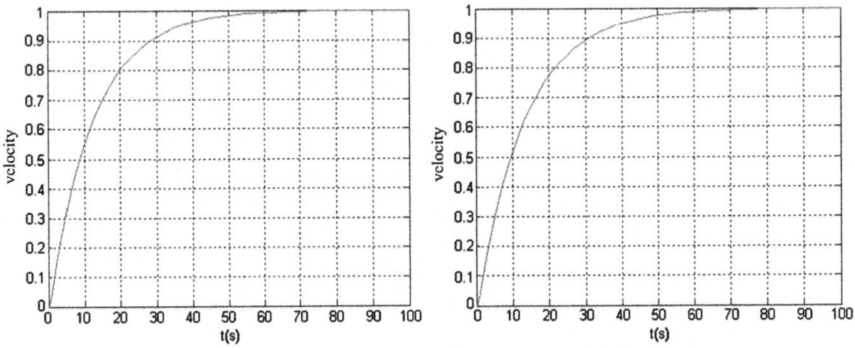


(a) $T_0^1 = 12.20s$ (b) $T_0^2 = 13.35s$

**Fig. 10.5** The simulated results with different time constants $T_0$

From (10.25), we can see that one of $T_1$ and $T_2$ is very large while the other is very small, and $t_1/t_2 = 0.32$, which means that the system function of Springrobot is a first-order model. Therefore, we have

$$T_0 = \frac{t_1 + t_2}{2.12} \approx 13.220. \tag{10.26}$$

Now, we can determine that the velocity model of the Springrobot is a first-order lag system with $T_0 \in [12.2\text{s}, 13.35\text{s}]$, $K_0 = 0.02$ and $\tau = 0.5$ s.

## 10.3 The Proposed Velocity Controller

### *10.3.1 Validating the Longitudinal Control System Function*

In Sect. 10.2, we identified the system model of Springrobot as the first-order lag system described as

$$H(s) = \frac{0.02}{T_0 s + 1} e^{-0.5s}, \tag{10.27}$$

where $T_0 \in [12.20\text{s}, 13.35\text{s}]$. The system responses for $T_0^1 = 12.20$ s and $T_0^2 = 13.35$ s are shown in Fig. 10.5.

We can estimate the accuracy of the system model. When $T_0^1 = 12.20$ s,

$$\begin{cases} \eta_1^1 = \frac{0.787-0.780}{0.780} \times 100\% \approx 0.897\%, & t = 20 \text{ s;} \\ \eta_1^2 = \frac{0.915-0.913}{0.915} \times 100\% \approx 0.219\%, & t = 30 \text{ s.} \end{cases} \tag{10.28}$$

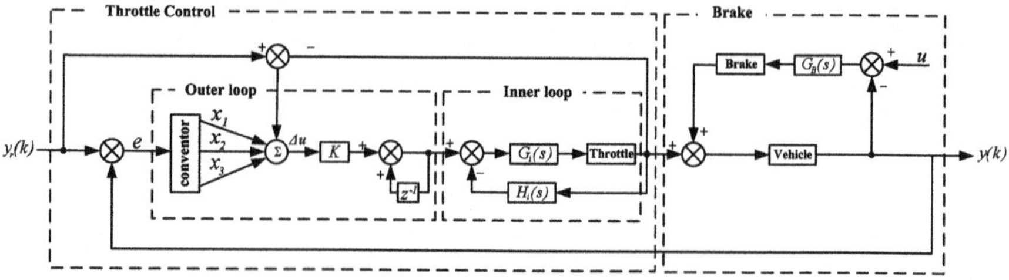


**Fig. 10.6** The structure of the velocity control system

When $T_0^2 = 13.35$ s,

$$\begin{cases} \eta_2^1 = \frac{0.780-0.765}{0.780} \times 100\% \approx 1.932\%, & t = 20 \text{ s}; \\ \eta_2^2 = \frac{0.915-0.886}{0.915} \times 100\% \approx 3.169\%, & t = 30 \text{ s}. \end{cases} \tag{10.29}$$

Upon the previous analysis, we can see that the system with $T_0 = 12.20$ s is better than that with $T_0 = 13.35$ s. Hence, the system function of the longitudinal system is described as

$$H(s) = \frac{0.02}{12.20s + 1} e^{-0.5s}. \tag{10.30}$$

## 10.3.2 Velocity Controller Design

The proposed velocity controller adopts a cascade control scheme combining throttle control and brake control (shown in Fig. 10.6), where the inner loop is a fuzzy adaptive robust control module and its outer loop is an improved Single-Neuron adaptive PID (SN-PID) control module based on the quadratic performance index. This velocity controller is capable of enduring environment change though its structure is simple. As a result, it is robust with respect to complex environment. We introduce the SN-PID below since it plays an important role in our system. Jetal et al. proposed the SN-PID thanks to self-learning and self-adaptation properties of a single neuron [2]. The SN-PID not only has a simple structure, but also adapts to environment change. Its structure is shown in Fig. 10.7, where $y_r(k)$ and $y(k)$ are its input and output variables; $x_1(k)$, $x_2(k)$, and $x_3(k)$ are the outputs of the converter,

$$\begin{cases} x_1(k) = y_r(k) - y(k) = e(k), \\ x_2(k) = e(k) - e(k-1) = \Delta e(k), \\ x_3(k) = e(k) - 2e(k-1) + e(k-2) = \Delta e(k) - \Delta e(k-1), \end{cases} \tag{10.31}$$

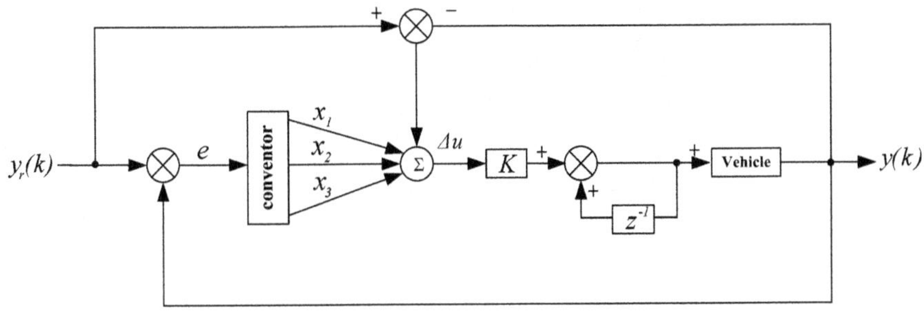


**Fig. 10.7** The control structure of the SN-PID

$K > 0$ is a proportionality factor of the neuron. Hence, the SN-PID control algorithm is described as

$$\Delta u(k) = u(k) - u(k-1) = K \sum_{i=1}^{3} \omega_i(k) x_i(k), \tag{10.32}$$

where $\omega_i(k)$ is the weight of $x_i(k)$. We would like to point out that both $K$ and $\omega_i(k)$ can be adjusted by self-learning. There are many different parameter learning rules each corresponding to different control algorithms. Here, we adopt the quadratic performance index to learn those parameters, namely

$$E = \frac{1}{2} P \left[ y_r(k+d) - y(k+d) \right]^2 + Q \nabla u^2(k), \tag{10.33}$$

where $d$ is the delay time; $P$ is the weight of output error; $Q$ is the weight of control increments.

Assume the system equation is formulated as

$$y(k+d) = -\sum_{i=1}^{n_a} a_i y(k+d-i) + \sum_{i=0}^{n_b} b_i u(k-i). \tag{10.34}$$

The weight update is in the direction of the negative gradient of $E$ in (10.33).

$$\nabla \omega_i(k) = \omega_i(k+1) - \omega_i(k) = -\eta_i \frac{\partial E}{\partial \omega_i(k)} \tag{10.35}$$

$$= \eta_i K \left\{ P b_0 e(k+d) x_i(k) - QK \left[ \sum_{i=1}^{3} \omega_i(k) x_i(k) \right] x_i(k) \right\}, \tag{10.36}$$

where $b_0$ is the response of a unit step function at the initial zero-state, and can be obtained by experiments.

Therefore, we obtain the following equations

$$u(k) = u(k-1) + K \sum_{i=1}^{3} \overline{\omega}_i(k) x_i(k),$$

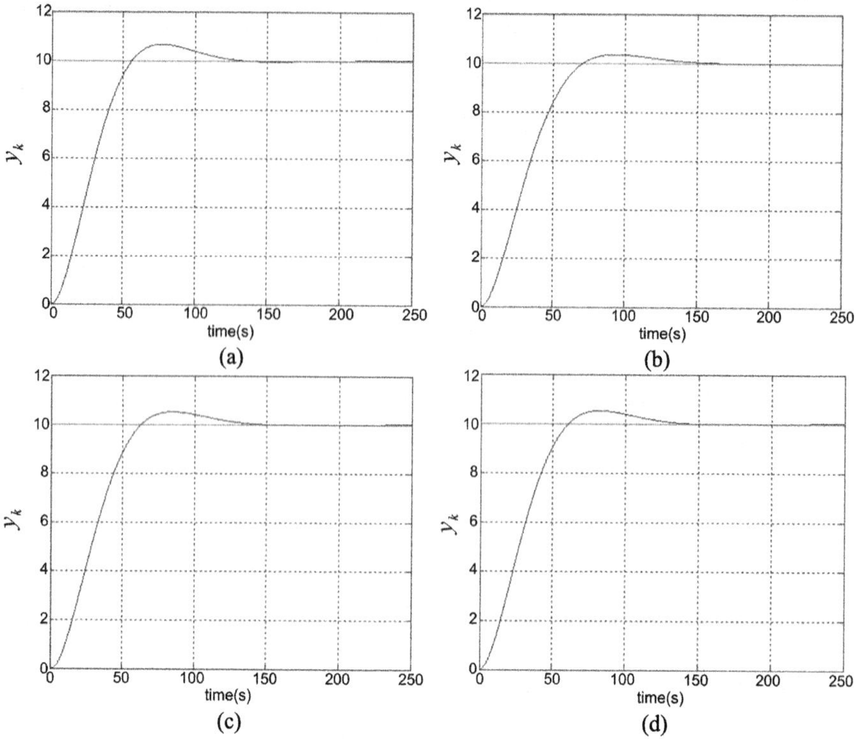


**Fig. 10.8** The simulation of speed: (**a**) unsupervised Hebb learning rule; (**b**) supervised Delta learning rule; (**c**) supervised Hebb learning rule; (**d**) improved Hebb learning rule

$$\overline{\omega}_i(k) = \frac{\omega_i(k)}{\sum_{i=1}^{3} |\omega_i(k)|},$$

$$\omega_i(k+1) = \omega_i(k) + \eta_i K \left\{ P b_0 e(k+d) x_i(k) - QK \left[ \sum_{j=1}^{3} \omega_j(k) x_j(k) \right] x_i(k) \right\}.$$

In practice, we use $e(k)$ instead of $e(k+d)$ due to $e(k+d)$ being unavailable.

## 10.4 Experimental Results and Analysis

We validate the longitudinal system model using four learning rules: unsupervised Hebb learning rule, supervised Delta learning rule, supervised Hebb learning rule, and improved Hebb learning rule. In our experiments, $n_P = 2$, $n_I = 0.4$, $n_D = 0.5$; $K$ is taken as 0.005, 0.075, 0.0045, and 0.085 in the four learning rules. The experimental results are shown in Figs. 10.8 and 10.9. From the experimental results, we can see that the value of $K$ affects the performance of the controller, for example, its response time and overshoot. Furthermore, we validate the SN-PID based on

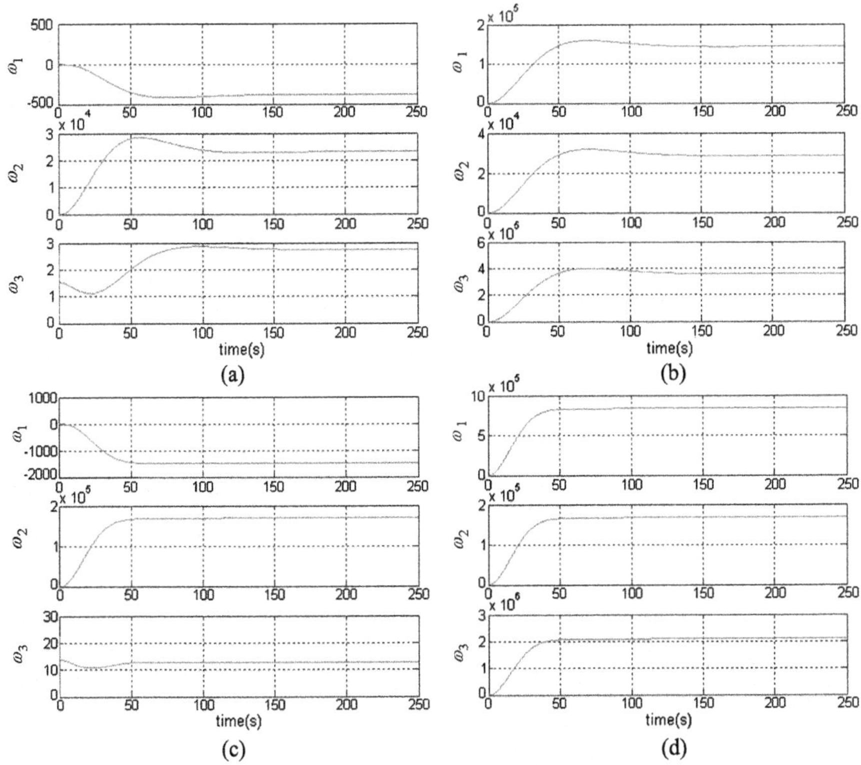


**Fig. 10.9** Weights vary with different learning rules: (**a**) unsupervised Hebb learning rule; (**b**) supervised Delta learning rule; (**c**) supervised Hebb learning rule; (**d**) improved Hebb learning rule

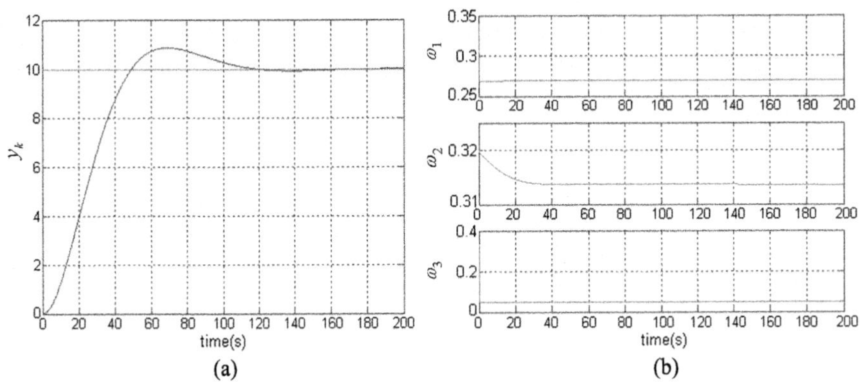


**Fig. 10.10** The SN-PID based on the quadratic performance index: (**a**) speed tracking; (**b**) different weights

the quadratic performance index, shown in Fig. 10.10. In this experiment, $P = 2$, $Q = 1$, $b_0 = 6$, $K = 0.02$, $n_P = 80$, $n_I = 0.4$, and $n_D = 259$. Compared to other learning rules, this learning rule has a lower computing burden and clearer physical meaning.

## References


1. Hou, Y.: The key control technologies of intelligent vehicles. Master Thesis, Xi'an Jiaotong University (2006)
2. Hunt, K.J., Sbarbaro, D., Zbikowski, R., Gawthrop, P.: Neural networks for control systems—a survey. Automatica **28**(6), 1083–1112 (1992)
3. Kim, J.H., Hayakawa, S., Suzuki, T., Hayashi, K., Okuma, S., Tsuchida, N., Shimizu, M., Kido, S.: Modeling of driver's collision avoidance maneuver based on controller switching model. IEEE Trans. Syst. Man Cybern., Part B, Cybern. **35**(6), 1131–1143 (2005)
4. Li, L., Wang, F.Y., Zhou, Q.: Integrated longitudinal and lateral tire/road friction modeling and monitoring for vehicle motion control. IEEE Trans. Intell. Transp. Syst. **7**(1), 1–19 (2006)
5. Nobe, S.A., Wang, F.Y.: An overview of recent developments in automated lateral and longitudinal vehicle controls. In: IEEE International Conference on Systems, Man, and Cybernetics (2001)
6. Pomerleau, D.A.: Neural network perception for mobile robot guidance. Technical report, DTIC Document (1992)
7. Pomerleau, D.A.: Progress in neural network-based vision for autonomous robot driving. In: Proc. of the Intelligent Vehicles '92 Symposium (1992)
8. Shladover, S.E., Desoer, C.A., Hedrick, J.K., Tomizuka, M., Walrand, J., Zhang, W.B., McMahon, D.H., Peng, H., Sheikholeslam, S., McKeown, N.: Automated vehicle control developments in the PATH program. IEEE Trans. Veh. Technol. **40**(1), 114–130 (1991)
9. Tamura, K., Furukawa, Y.: Autonomous vehicle control system of ICVS City Pal: electrical tow-bar function. In: Proc. of the IEEE International Conference on Intelligent Vehicles Symposium (2000)
10. Tanaka, K., Kosaki, T.: Design of a stable fuzzy controller for an articulated vehicle. IEEE Trans. Syst. Man Cybern., Part B, Cybern. **27**(3), 552–558 (1997)
11. Tanaka, K., Kosaki, T., Wang, H.O.: Backing control problem of a mobile robot with multiple trailers: fuzzy modeling and LMI-based design. IEEE Trans. Syst. Man Cybern., Part C, Appl. Rev. **28**(3), 329–337 (1998)
12. Tanaka, K., Sugeno, M.: Stability analysis of fuzzy systems using Lyapunov's direct method. In: Proc. NAFIPS, pp. 133–136 (1990)
13. Tanaka, K., Sugeno, M.: Stability analysis and design of fuzzy control systems. Fuzzy Sets Syst. **45**(2), 135–156 (1992)

# Index




H. Cheng, *Autonomous Intelligent Vehicles*,
Advances in Computer Vision and Pattern Recognition,
DOI 10.1007/978-1-4471-2280-7,

CPSIA information can be obtained
at www.ICGtesting.com
Printed in the USA
LVOW02*1112301115
464660LV00001B/38/P

9 781447 122791